LOW CHOLESTEROL COOKBOOK

1500 DAYS EASY AND TASTY RECIPES TO REDUCE YOUR BAD CHOLESTEROL LEVEL |

30 DAYS MEAL PLAN TO GET RID STRESS AND IMPROVE YOUR HEART HEALT

Abigail Parker

Table of Contents

INTRODUCTION

People all over the world are now turning towards healthier lifestyles. Low cholesterol is one of the goals that has caught on like wildfire. Low cholesterol can be achieved by eating the right type of foods, such as leafy greens, whole grains, beans, and fish. Furthermore, a low-cholesterol diet typically contains limited amounts of saturated fat, cholesterol, and sodium. More specifically, the Mayo Clinic notes that a low-cholesterol diet includes at least 5 to 10 servings of fruits and vegetables per day, plus 25 to 35 grams of fiber per day. With this information in mind, a cookbook that follows the principles of a low-cholesterol diet can be invaluable for those looking to maintain a healthy lifestyle.

Eating these kinds of foods can help people lower their cholesterol levels, reduce their risk of heart disease, and lose weight. This is why the Low Cholesterol Cookbook was created, to provide nutritious and delicious recipes that are low in cholesterol. In this cookbook, you will find an array of meals and snacks that are healthy, mouthwatering, and easy to prepare. With the wide variety of recipes available, you can create a healthier lifestyle that you can enjoy for years to come.

Each recipe is designed to include plenty of helpful nutrition information and only contains good ingredients that are low in cholesterol. This makes it easier for you to create meals and snacks that will help you stay on track with your low-cholesterol goals.

WHAT IS CHOLESTEROL?

Cholesterol is an essential element of the human body, yet when individuals have an imbalance of cholesterol their health can be put in jeopardy. To better understand cholesterol and its effects on the body, it is important to look at what cholesterol is, what causes it to be out of balance and the potential effects of an imbalance. By learning the basics, individuals can create a plan to make sure that their cholesterol remains within a healthy range.

Cholesterol is a type of fat that is present in the bloodstream and in foods such as dairy products, eggs and red meat. The body produces cholesterol naturally and needs it to build cell walls, hormones, and other substances. Too much cholesterol in the blood, however, can be dangerous and increase a person's risk of heart disease, stroke, and other related conditions.

When individuals have an imbalance of cholesterol, it can affect how much cholesterol is being produced and distributed throughout the body. To provide the body with the cholesterol it needs, the liver will process cholesterol from the food, along with producing its own. When there is an excess of cholesterol in the body, it will accumulate in the arteries and lead to health problems such as arteriosclerosis, heart disease, stroke and other related conditions. To maintain a healthy cholesterol balance, doctors often recommend a heart-healthy diet that is low in saturated fat and cholesterol. This type of diet should also be supplemented with regular exercise, which has been proven to help reduce bad cholesterol levels. By balancing diet and exercise, individuals can ensure that their cholesterol levels remain healthy and in balance.

Bad And Good Cholesterol

There are two different types of cholesterol: high-density lipoprotein, and low-density lipoprotein. The body needs a certain amount of these two types in order to remain healthy; too much of either can be dangerous.

1. **High Density Lipoprotein:** It is considered the "good" cholesterol because it helps remove too much cholesterol from the body. It binds to the fatty substances in the arteries and then carries them back to the liver, which then breaks them down. HDL also helps keep the walls of the arteries strong and flexible, which reduces the risk of heart disease and stroke. Additionally, HDL has anti-inflammatory properties which can help reduce arterial plaque build-up and protect against heart attack or other cardiovascular events.

2. **Low Density Lipoprotein:** Low density lipoprotein, or LDL, is known as the "bad" cholesterol as it puts individuals at risk for heart disease and stroke. Too much LDL in the body can clog the arteries, leading to a buildup of plaque which can cause hardening of the arteries and make it difficult for oxygen and other nutrients to reach the body's organs.

To ensure that LDL levels are kept low, doctors typically recommend reducing intake of saturated and trans fats, balance diet with plenty of fresh fruits, vegetables, and whole grains, and increasing exercise. Additionally, cutting back on red meat and processed foods is beneficial when trying to maintain low levels of LDL.

It is important to keep track of one's cholesterol levels and make sure that the HDL and LDL levels are within a healthy range. If it is found that one's cholesterol is too high, a visit to a doctor may be necessary in order to discuss lifestyle changes, medications and other treatment options. Making lifestyle changes such as increasing physical activity, quitting smoking, eating a balanced diet, managing stress and avoiding foods high in fat and cholesterol can help reduce one's risk of having an imbalance in cholesterol levels. By understanding cholesterol and taking steps to maintain balance, individuals can improve their overall health and reduce their risk of developing health conditions related to an imbalance.

Symptoms Of High Cholesterol Level

High cholesterol levels do not usually cause any overt medical signs or symptoms, so individuals may not be aware that their cholesterol is too high. The most common symptom experienced by those with high cholesterol is chest pain due to decreased blood flow to the heart caused by hardened arteries. Other symptoms of high cholesterol levels include shortness of breath, numbness in the legs and feet, recurrent headaches, dizziness, and irregular heartbeats. In extreme cases, high cholesterol levels can lead to stroke and even heart attack.

It is crucial to regularly monitor one's cholesterol levels in order to identify any issues early on and take steps to rectify the situation. Regular lab tests should be done to check for an imbalance of LDL and HDL levels. If levels are higher than expected, consulting a doctor is recommended in order to identify what steps need to be taken to bring them back into balance.

Causes Of High Cholesterol Level

High cholesterol levels can be the result of a genetic disposition, lifestyle choices, or a combination of the two. Factors such as an unhealthy diet, lack of physical activity, diabetes, smoking, and obesity can contribute to an increase in LDL levels and a decrease in HDL levels. Certain medications and medical conditions can also affect one's cholesterol levels; thus, if any of these risk factors are present, it is important to be aware of the potential consequences. Furthermore, age is another factor that affects cholesterol levels; as individuals age, their cholesterol levels tend to increase due to the natural changes that occur in the body over time.

High cholesterol can have serious implications for an individual's health and well-being, so it is critical to make sure that levels are kept in check. No matter one's age, gender or genetic background, it is important to be aware of the risk factors associated with cholesterol and make smart lifestyle choices in order to ensure that levels remain within a healthy range.

HOW TO LOWER YOUR CHOLESTEROL LEVEL

Lowering cholesterol levels requires making small lifestyle changes such as reducing consumption of processed foods, saturated fats and trans fats, increasing physical activity and exercising regularly, drinking alcohol in moderation, eating more fiber from whole grains and fresh fruits and vegetables, avoiding high sugar foods, and quitting smoking. In addition to lifestyle changes, it is also advisable to have regular checkups with a doctor to monitor one's cholesterol level and make sure it stays in the healthy range. With the right lifestyle adjustments, individuals can keep their cholesterol in balance and live a healthier life.

Recommended Exercise

Regular physical activity and exercise are essential for controlling cholesterol levels and maintaining overall health. A minimum of 30 minutes of moderate exercise most days of the week is recommended for individuals with high cholesterol levels. Low impact exercises, such as walking, swimming, and cycling can help to reduce levels while helping to improve circulation, decrease levels of stress and increase energy. Additionally, individuals should aim to include strength-training exercises into their routine two to three times per week.

Strength-training exercises help to build muscle, boost metabolism, increase fat burn and build endurance. Taking the time to add physical activity into one's lifestyle can be a rewarding experience and result in improved overall health and happiness. Regular physical activity is an important part of reducing cholesterol and maintaining homeostasis in the body. With the right lifestyle changes, it is possible to lower cholesterol and stay healthy for many years to come.

Foods to Eat

Eating healthy and reducing cholesterol levels go hand in hand. Making smart choices when it comes to food can be particularly beneficial for people with high cholesterol. These includes:

Eating more fiber- Dietary fiber is divided into two types: soluble and insoluble fiber. Soluble fiber is important for lowering LDL cholesterol levels since it dissolves in water. It works by absorbing bile salts in the intestines. To make additional bile salts, the body removes cholesterol from the circulation. It's critical to consume 5 to 10 grams of soluble fiber every day.

Fruits, vegetables, whole grains, and legumes are high in dietary fiber. Oat bran, strawberries, apples, citrus fruit, barley, beans, rice bran, and peas are high in soluble fiber. Most whole grains, carrots, cauliflower, apple peel, and beetrootss include insoluble fiber, which may help you feel full and keep you regular but not affect cholesterol.

Opting for healthy fats- Switching to monounsaturated or polyunsaturated fats instead of saturated and trans fats can help to reduce cholesterol levels and overall improve one's health. Extra-virgin olive oil, unrefined safflower oil, almonds, and avocados should all be included in your diet. Omega-3 fatty acids, which may be found in walnuts, tofu, soybeans, fatty fish, and flaxseed, are healthy fats to consume.

Choosing lean proteins- Healthy proteins are a key component of healthy cholesterol levels. To reduce fat and cholesterol content, individuals should opt for lean proteins that are low in saturated fat. This includes skinless chicken, fish, eggs, and ground turkey. Plant-based proteins, such as tofu and tempeh, are also a healthful option that can substitute for animal proteins.

Incorporating beans and legumes- These powerhouse foods are packed with fiber, protein, vitamins, and minerals. Incorporating them into the diet on a regular basis has been linked to improved cholesterol levels. Some suggestions include black beans, kidney beans, garbanzo beans, lentils, and pinto beans. Consuming legumes and beans in place of animal proteins can help to increase fiber and reduce saturated fat intake.

Foods To Avoid

If you are trying to lower cholesterol and triglycerides, there are several things to avoid. Processed meats, fast foods and foods containing trans fats should be avoided. Also, reduce the number of sugary foods you eat and the amount of sugar in the dishes you currently eat. Most recipes can still be made with half to two-thirds of the specified sugar. Here are some details:

Saturated Fats- High cholesterol levels are mostly caused by saturated fats. Saturated fats, in general, are solid fats at room temperature. Saturated fats are categorized into many types, and the amount of saturated fat in packaged goods in the United States is listed on the nutrition information label. This suggests that you have perfect control over the amount of saturated fat you eat. The American Heart Association and others recommend that you consume no more than 20 grams of saturated fat each day. The recipes in this book will guide you to the cuts of meat and cooking techniques necessary to reach your aim.

Red Meats- Beef, hog, and lamb are frequently the highest in saturated fat. They do, in fact, have more than fish or poultry. The quantity they have, however, is significantly depending on the cut you select. High-fat beef cuts may contain up to five times as much saturated fat as lean cuts.

Poultry Skin- While poultry skin may not contain as much saturated fat as red meat, it does include a significant amount. A chicken thigh with skin contains nearly 2 g more saturated fat than a chicken thigh with only the flesh. And getting rid of the fat in this case is simple—just don't eat the skin.

Whole-Milk Dairy- Another category where making informed decisions might help reduce saturated fat intake is dairy products. Avoid goods containing whole milk or cream. Choose fat-free sour cream and cream cheese, skim milk, and low-fat cheeses. Use fat-free evaporated milk instead of cream.

Tropical Oils- Some of the plant oils in this category contain saturated fats. Among them are palm, palm kernel, and coconut oils, as well as cocoa butter. Although they are usually easy to avoid, certain commercial baked goods and processed meals may include them.

Trans Fats- Trans fats are also known as trans-fatty acids. They are created through the hydrogenation of hydrogen and vegetable oil. As a result, the fat becomes more firm and less prone to deterioration. Trans fats are still widely used in commercially baked goods and fried foods. Food manufacturers must include trans fat content on nutrition labels. The amount on the food label is less than 0.5 grams per serving, maybe 0 grams trans-fat.

Margarine and Other Hydrogenated Oils- Avoid margarine and solid shortening that include hydrogenated or partially hydrogenated oils. Although some of the recipes in this book call for margarine due to the texture of the food, liquid or soft margarine should be used wherever possible.

Commercial Baked Goods and Fried Foods- Read product labels and be aware that hydrogenated oils are commonly used in baked goods. Although public awareness has grown and many restaurants now use trans fat-free oils, be sure you know what you're eating.

Egg Yolks- One egg yolk has 214 mg of cholesterol, which is more than two-thirds of the daily allowance. You can't use egg substitutes or egg whites in place of whole eggs.

BREAKFAST RECIPES

TOFU SCRAMBLE WITH TOMATO AND SPINACH

SERVINGS	PREPARATION TIME	COOKING TIME
2	10 Mins	13 Mins

Ingredients

- ·2 tsp (30ml) olive oil
- ·¼ cup (30g) chopped sweet onion
- ·1 cup (125g) halved cherry tomatoes
- ·1 cup (30) fresh baby spinach
- ·10 oz (280g) firm tofu, crumbled into small pieces
- ·¼ cup (60g) low-fat cottage cheese
- ·1 tsp (1g) chopped fresh oregano
- ·Sea salt & ground black pepper

Directions

1.Warm the olive oil in a medium nonstick skillet over medium heat.
2.Add the onion to the pan and sauté for 3 minutes until translucent. Add the tomatoes and spinach, then sauté for 3 minutes until the spinach is wilted.
3.Add the tofu to the skillet and gently stir using a rubber spatula for 7 minutes until warm. Fold in the cottage cheese and oregano. Season with salt and pepper and serve.

 NUTRITIONAL VALUE

Kcal	Carbs	Protein	Total Fat	Sat. Fat	Cholesterol
201	9g	20g	5g	1g	2mg

CRANBERRY ORANGE MIXED GRAIN GRANOLA

SERVINGS
2

PREPARATION TIME
5 Mins

COOKING TIME
20 Mins

Ingredients

- ·1/2 cup (50g) regular rolled oats
- ·1/4 cup (25g) barley flakes
- ·1/2 cup (50g) Kamut flakes or corn or wheat flakes
- ·1/8 cup (20g) sunflower seeds
- ·1 1/2 tbsp (20ml) pure maple syrup
- ·1/2 tbsp (7ml) safflower oil
- ·1/2 tbsp (7ml) orange juice
- ·1/2 tsp (2ml) vanilla extract
- ·1 tsp (2g) fresh orange zest
- ·1/4 cup (30g) chopped dried cranberries

Directions

1.Preheat the oven to 350°F (180°C).
2.Combine the rolled oats, barley, Kamut, and sunflower seeds in a large bowl.
3.In a small bowl, combine the maple syrup, safflower oil, orange juice, vanilla, and orange zest.
4.Drizzle the maple syrup mixture over the grains and toss to coat. Spread the mixture on a baking sheet.
5.Bake within 15 to 20 minutes, stirring once until the mixture is lightly toasted.
6.Stir in the cranberries, let the granola cool completely, and store in an airtight container at room temperature for up to 1 week.

 NUTRITIONAL VALUE

Kcal	Carbs	Protein	Total Fat	Sat. Fat	Cholesterol
226	39g	5g	8g	1g	0mg

HONEY RICE PUDDING

SERVINGS	PREPARATION TIME	COOKING TIME
2	10 Mins	20 Mins

Ingredients

- ·½ cup (100g) brown basmati rice
- ·2 cups (475ml) water
- ·1 cup (240ml) unsweetened nondairy milk (soy, almond, rice), + extra for serving
- ·1 tsp (1ml) pure vanilla extract
- ·⅛ tsp ground cinnamon
- ·Pinch of sea salt
- ·¼ cup (50g) dried unsweetened cranberries
- ·¼ cup (30g) chopped pistachios
- ·2 tbsp (30ml) honey

Directions

1.Place the rice in a bowl and add the water. Soak overnight in the refrigerator, then drain.

2.Stir the rice, water, milk, vanilla, cinnamon, and salt in a medium saucepan and place over medium heat.

3.Boil the mixture and adjust to low heat. Simmer for 20 minutes until the rice is tender and the liquid is almost absorbed, stirring frequently.

4.Remove the saucepan and stir in the cranberries, pistachios, and honey. Add more non-dairy milk if you like thinner pudding. Serve.

 NUTRITIONAL VALUE

Kcal	Carbs	Protein	Total Fat	Sat. Fat	Cholesterol
341	64g	6g	8g	0g	0mg

PUMPKIN OATMEAL SMOOTHIES

SERVINGS
2

PREPARATION TIME
5 Mins

COOKING TIME
0 Mins

Ingredients

- ·2 cups (475ml) unsweetened soy milk
- ·1 cup (230g) puréed canned pumpkin
- ·½ cup (50g) rolled oats
- ·1 tbsp (30g) hemp hearts
- ·1 tbsp (30ml) blackstrap black
- treacle
  ·¼ tsp ground
- cinnamon
  ·⅛ tsp (0,3g) ground
- nutmeg
  ·⅛ tsp (0,3g) ground ginger

Directions

1.In a blender, add the soy milk, pumpkin, oats, hemp hearts, treacle, cinnamon, nutmeg, and ginger and purée until smooth.
2.Pour into glasses and serve immediately.

 NUTRITIONAL VALUE

Kcal	Carbs	Protein	Total Fat	Sat. Fat	Cholesterol
332	47g	15g	9g	1g	0mg

BLUEBERRY ALMOND BREAKFAST BOWL

SERVINGS	PREPARATION TIME	COOKING TIME
2	15 Mins	0 Mins

Ingredients

- ·1 1/2 cup (375g) full-fat plain Greek yogurt
- ·1/2 cup (100g) blueberries, divided
- ·1 small banana, cut into slices
- ·2 tbsp (30g) chia seeds
- ·4 tbsp (60ml) low-fat almond milk
- ·2 tbsp (30g) sliced almonds, toasted

Directions

1.In your blender, blend the yogurt, ¼ cup of the blueberries, the banana, chia seeds, and almond milk until smooth.

2.Spoon into a cereal bowl and top with the almonds and remaining blueberries.

 NUTRITIONAL VALUE

Kcal	Carbs	Protein	Total Fat	Sat. Fat	Cholesterol
343	44g	12g	15g	5g	24mg

AMARANTH AND DATE PORRIDGE

SERVINGS

2

PREPARATION TIME

5 Mins

COOKING TIME

20-22 Mins

Ingredients

- ·1/2 cup (100g) amaranth
- ·1 1/4 cup (300ml) water
- ·1/4 cup (60ml) unsweetened apple juice
- ·½ tbsp (15ml) pure maple syrup
- ·1/2 tsp (2ml) sunflower oil
- ·⅛ tsp (0,3g) ground nutmeg
- ·Pinch of salt
- ·1/8 cup (15g) Medjool dates, pitted and chopped

Directions

1.In a medium saucepan, combine the amaranth, water, apple juice, maple syrup, sunflower oil, nutmeg, and salt.

2.Let it boil over medium heat, reduce heat to low, and simmer within 15 minutes, stirring occasionally. Stir the mixture and add the dates.

3.Continue cooking within 5 to 7 minutes, stirring frequently, or until the porridge is thickened and the amaranth is tender. Serve immediately.

 NUTRITIONAL VALUE

Kcal	Carbs	Protein	Total Fat	Sat. Fat	Cholesterol
252	47g	7g	5g	1g	0mg

CURRIED FARRO HOT CEREAL

SERVINGS	PREPARATION TIME	COOKING TIME
2	10 Mins	25-27 Mins

Ingredients

- ·1/2 cup (50g) farro
- ·1/4 cup (60ml) unsweetened apple juice
- ·3/4 cups (180ml) water
- ·1/4 cup (60ml) of low-fat soy milk
- ·½ tbsp (8ml) pure maple syrup, + more for serving (optional)
- ·1 tsp (3g) curry powder
- ·Pinch salt
- ·1/8 cup (15g) dried currants

Directions

1.In a medium-heavy saucepan, combine the farro, apple juice, water, soy milk, maple syrup, curry powder, and salt. Let it simmer over medium heat, then adjust to low heat.

2.Cover the pot and cook the farro mixture for 20 minutes, stirring occasionally. Stir in the currants and cook for 5 to 7 minutes or until the grains are tender but still chewy.

3.Serve with fresh fruit and a drizzle of maple syrup, if desired.

 NUTRITIONAL VALUE

Kcal	Carbs	Protein	Total Fat	Sat. Fat	Cholesterol
182	38g	5g	2g	0g	0mg

BERRY, KALE, AND CHIA SMOOTHIES

SERVINGS
2

PREPARATION TIME
5 Mins

COOKING TIME
0 Mins

Ingredients

- ·1½ cups (350ml) unsweetened soy milk
- ·1 cup (30g) roughly chopped kale
- ·1 cup (120g) berries (blueberries, strawberries, raspberries, or blackberries)
- ·2 tbsp (30g) chia seeds
- ·2 tbsp (50ml) honey
- ·⅛ tsp (0,3g) ground nutmeg

Directions

1.Add the milk, kale, berries, chia seeds, honey, and nutmeg in your blender and blend until very smooth.
2.Pour into glasses and serve immediately.

 NUTRITIONAL VALUE

Kcal	Carbs	Protein	Total Fat	Sat. Fat	Cholesterol
253	36g	6g	9g	1g	0mg

SCRAMBLED EGG TACOS

SERVINGS

2

PREPARATION TIME

10 Mins

COOKING TIME

10 Mins

Ingredients

- ·1 whole egg
- ·3 egg whites
- ·½ tbsp (15ml) water
- ·1 tsp (3g) chili powder
- ·Pinch of salt, black pepper, & red pepper flakes
- ·½ tsp (3ml) olive oil
- ·2 warmed crisp corn taco shells or 2 warmed corn or flour tortillas
- ·1/8 cup (30ml) salsa
- ·¼ cup (30g) frozen corn, thawed
- ·1 tbsp (25g) grated feta cheese
- ·1/2 cup (15g) shredded cos lettuce

Directions

1.In your medium bowl, combine the egg, egg whites, water, chili powder, salt, pepper, and red pepper flakes, and beat thoroughly with a fork until foamy.

2.Heat the olive oil in your medium skillet over medium heat. Add the egg mixture and cook for 5 to 7 minutes, frequently stirring, until the eggs are cooked through. Remove from the heat.

3.Meanwhile, warm the taco shells as directed on the package. Divide the egg mixture among the taco shells and top with the salsa, corn, cheese, and lettuce. Serve immediately.

 NUTRITIONAL VALUE

Kcal	Carbs	Protein	Total Fat	Sat. Fat	Cholesterol
166	24g	11g	4g	1g	56mg

ASPARAGUS KALE FRITTATA

SERVINGS
2

PREPARATION TIME
10 Mins

COOKING TIME
15 Mins

Ingredients

- ·1 small bunch of curly kale
- ·1 tsp (5ml) olive oil
- ·8 asparagus spears, cut into 2-inch (5cm) pieces
- ·2 tbsp (60ml) water
- ·1 whole egg
- ·5 egg whites
- ·1 tbsp (30g) low-fat Greek yogurt
- ·½ tsp (0,5g) dried thyme leaves
- ·Pinch salt
- ·⅛ tsp (0,2g) white pepper
- ·Pinch turmeric
- ·2 tbsp (50g) crumbled goat cheese

Directions

1.Rinse the kale thoroughly and remove the tough center stem. Tear into bite-sized pieces.

2.Heat a 9-inch skillet over medium heat and add the olive oil.

3.When the oil is hot, add the kale and asparagus and sauté for 3 minutes, stirring frequently. Add the water, cover the pan, and steam for 2 minutes.

4.Meanwhile, in your medium bowl, beat the egg, egg whites, yogurt, thyme, salt, pepper, and turmeric. Stir in the cheese.

5.Uncover the pan and add the egg mixture to the vegetables. Cook over medium heat within 10 minutes until the eggs are set. Serve immediately.

 NUTRITIONAL VALUE

Kcal	Carbs	Protein	Total Fat	Sat. Fat	Cholesterol
120	9g	12g	5g	2g	73mg

NUTTY RICE WAFFLES

SERVINGS
2

PREPARATION TIME
10 Mins

COOKING TIME
5 Mins

Ingredients

- ·1/2 cup (60g) brown rice flour
- ·3/4 tsp (4g) baking powder
- ·1/2 tsp (1g) ground cinnamon
- ·⅛ tsp (0,3g) ground nutmeg
- ·Pinch of salt
- ·1 egg, separated
- ·1/4 cup (60ml) almond or soy milk
- ·1 tbsp (30ml) honey or pure maple syrup
- ·1/2 tsp (2g) vanilla extract
- ·1 1/2 tbsp (30g) ground pecans

Directions

1.Mix the brown rice flour, baking powder, cinnamon, nutmeg, and salt in a medium bowl. In your small bowl, combine the egg yolk, almond milk, honey, and vanilla.

2.In another medium bowl, beat the egg white until stiff. Stir the egg yolk mixture into the dry ingredients, then fold the egg white.

3.Preheat a waffle iron and spray it with nonstick cooking spray. Add batter to the waffle iron per the manufacturer's instructions. Close the iron and cook for 4 to 5 minutes until the steaming stops.

4.Remove the waffle from the iron, sprinkle with ground pecans, and serve immediately.

 NUTRITIONAL VALUE

Kcal	Carbs	Protein	Total Fat	Sat. Fat	Cholesterol
95	30g	6g	7g	1g	53mg

GREEN TEA AND RASPBERRY SMOOTHIES

SERVINGS
2

PREPARATION TIME
10 Mins
+sleeping & cooling time

COOKING TIME
0 Mins

Ingredients

- ·1 green tea bag
- ·½ cup (120ml) boiling water
- ·2 cups (475ml) unsweetened vanilla almond or soy milk
- ·2 cups (250g) frozen raspberries
- ·1 courgette, cut into chunks
- ·2 tbsp (60ml) honey
- ·½ tsp (1gr) chopped fresh mint

Directions

1. In a mug, steep the tea bag in boiling water for 4 to 5 minutes.
2. Remove the bag, squeeze it out into the mug, and place the tea in the refrigerator for 45 minutes to cool completely.
3. Add the cooled tea, milk, raspberries, courgette, honey, and mint in a blender and blend until very smooth. Pour into glasses and serve immediately.

 NUTRITIONAL VALUE

Kcal	Carbs	Protein	Total Fat	Sat. Fat	Cholesterol
274	50g	11g	5g	1g	0mg

CINNAMON OAT BRAN BANANA PANCAKES

SERVINGS	**PREPARATION TIME**	**COOKING TIME**
2	15 Mins	4 Mins

Ingredients

- ·1/2 cup (60g) gluten-free flour blend
- ·1/8 cup (15g) oat bran
- ·1/2 tbsp (15g) brown sugar
- ·1/2 tsp (0,5g) ground cinnamon
- ·1/4 tsp (1g) bicarbonate of soda
- ·1/4 tsp (1g) baking powder
- ·Half of 1 small banana, peeled & mashed
- ·1/8 cup (30ml) of low-fat milk
- ·1 egg, separated
- ·1/2 tbsp (10ml) sunflower oil

Directions

1.Mix the flour, oat bran, brown sugar, cinnamon, bicarbonate of soda, and baking powder in your medium bowl with a wire whisk.

2.In another medium bowl, beat the banana, milk, and egg yolk. In another medium bowl, beat the egg white with your electric mixer until stiff peaks form.

3.Add the banana mixture to your flour mixture and stir just until combined. Do not overmix. Fold in the beaten egg white.

4.Heat your nonstick griddle or large skillet with the oil over medium heat, and swirl it around your pan.

5.Pour a scant ¼ cup of the batter onto the griddle. Repeat just to fill the pan.

6.Cook the pancakes for 2 minutes until the edges start to look lightly browned and bubbles form on the surface.

7.Flip the pancakes and cook for 1 to 2 minutes or until the bottoms are browned. Serve immediately.

 NUTRITIONAL VALUE

Kcal	Carbs	Protein	Total Fat	Sat. Fat	Cholesterol
245	44g	7g	6g	1g	55mg

ORANGE APRICOT MUESLI

SERVINGS

2

PREPARATION TIME

10 Mins

COOKING TIME

0 Mins

Ingredients

- ·1 cup (100g) regular rolled oats, toasted if desired
- ·1/8 cup (15g) oat bran
- ·1/8 cup (15g) dried chopped apricots
- ·1/8 cup (15g) chopped walnuts
- ·Pinch of salt
- ·1/2 teaspoon (0,5g) ground cinnamon
- ·1/8 cup (30ml) orange juice
- ·¾ cups (90ml) low-fat almond, soy, or dairy milk

Directions

1.In a medium bowl, combine the oats, oat bran, apricots, walnuts, salt, and cinnamon. Add the orange juice and milk and mix well.

2.You can let this stand for 10 minutes, then serve, or cover the bowl and refrigerate overnight, stirring gently before serving.

 NUTRITIONAL VALUE

Kcal	Carbs	Protein	Total Fat	Sat. Fat	Cholesterol
280	47g	9g	9g	1g	0mg

TEMPEH CAPRESE BREAKFAST SANDWICHES

SERVINGS
2

PREPARATION TIME
10 Mins

COOKING TIME
10 Mins

Ingredients

- ·4 slices dark rye bread
- ·3 tsp (15ml) olive oil, divided
- ·6 oz (170g) tempeh, cut into 2 slices
- ·1 large tomato, thinly sliced
- ·¼ cup (5g) shredded fresh basil
- ·½ cup (125g) fat-free shredded mozzarella
- ·Sea salt & ground black pepper to taste

Directions

1.Preheat the oven to 400°F (200°C). Line a baking sheet with parchment paper.

2.Brush both sides of each bread slice with 2 tsp olive oil and arrange the bread on the baking sheet. Toast the bread in the oven for 4 minutes until lightly browned and crispy, turning once.

3.In a medium skillet, warm the remaining olive oil over medium heat. Panfry the tempeh for 6 minutes until it is browned and crispy, turning once.

4.Remove the bread and remove the tempeh from the heat.

5.Place two slices of bread on a cutting board and top with the tempeh slices. Evenly divide the tomato slices, basil, and cheese onto the tempeh—season with salt and pepper.

6.Top with the remaining slices of bread and diagonally cut the sandwiches in half. Serve.

 NUTRITIONAL VALUE

Kcal	Carbs	Protein	Total Fat	Sat. Fat	Cholesterol
464	45g	30g	19g	3g	5mg

VEGAN & VEGETARIAN RECIPES

TOFU WITH CHIMICHURRI SAUCE

SERVINGS

2

PREPARATION TIME

15 Mins

COOKING TIME

10 Mins

Ingredients

- ·1/4 cup (5g) packed fresh parsley leaves
- ·1/8 cup (3g) packed fresh basil leaves
- · 1 1/2 tbsp (30g) fresh chopped chives
- ·1/2 tsp (2g) fresh oregano leaves
- ·1 scallion, chopped
- ·1 tbsp (30ml) lime juice
- ·1/2 tbsp (15ml) pure maple syrup
- ·1 clove of garlic
- ·1 tbsp (30ml) water
- ·Pinch of salt & red pepper flakes
- ·12 oz (340g) extra-firm tofu, drained
- ·½ tsp (3ml) olive oil
- ·½ tsp (2g) smoked paprika
- ·1/8 tsp (0,5g) ground turmeric

Directions

1.In a blender, blend the parsley, basil, chives, oregano, green onions, lime juice, maple syrup, garlic, water, red pepper flakes, and salt until the herbs are finely chopped. Set aside.

2.Press the tofu between sheets of paper towels to remove more moisture. Cut the tofu into 2 slices.

3.In a nonstick skillet, heat the olive oil over medium-high heat. Add the paprika and turmeric and stir well.

4.Add the tofu slices, and cook for 5 minutes on one side. Flip and cook for 5 minutes on the second side. Plate the tofu, drizzle with the chimichurri sauce, and serve immediately.

 NUTRITIONAL VALUE

Kcal	Carbs	Protein	Total Fat	Sat. Fat	Cholesterol
194	10g	18g	11g	1g	0mg

VEGETABLE LO MEIN

SERVINGS
2

PREPARATION TIME
15 Mins

COOKING TIME
11-15 Mins

Ingredients

- ·1/4 cup (60ml) low-sodium vegetable broth
- ·1/2 tbsp (15g) cornstarch
- ·1/2 tbsp (15ml) pure maple syrup
- ·½ tsp (3ml) low-sodium soy sauce
- ·½ tsp (3ml) hoisin sauce
- ·½ tsp (3ml) toasted sesame oil
- ·4-oz (110g) whole-wheat spaghetti
- ·1 tsp (5ml) olive oil
- ·4-oz (110g) sliced cremini mushrooms
- ·1 cup (90g) bite-sized broccoli florets
- ·1 clove of garlic, minced
- ·1 cup (100g) green beans, sliced into 1-inch (2,5cm) pieces
- ·1 cup (20g) chopped red cabbage
- ·Half (8-oz) (220g) can of no-salt-added cannellini beans, rinsed and drained

Directions

1.Heat your large pot of water to boiling.

2.Meanwhile, in your small bowl, whisk together the vegetable broth, cornstarch, maple syrup, soy sauce, hoisin sauce, and toasted sesame oil. Set aside.

3.Cook the spaghetti in your skillet with enough water for 6 minutes until just al dente; drain and set aside.

4.Heat the olive oil in your large nonstick skillet over medium-high heat .

5.Add the mushrooms, broccoli, garlic, green beans, and red cabbage. Stir-fry for 3 to 5 minutes or until the vegetables are crisp-tender.

6.Add the cooked spaghetti and cannellini beans to the skillet, and stir-fry for 1 minute. Add the sauce and stir-fry for 1 to 2 minutes or until the sauce thickens slightly. Serve immediately.

 NUTRITIONAL VALUE

Kcal	Carbs	Protein	Total Fat	Sat. Fat	Cholesterol
455	86g	22g	5g	1g	0mg

SEITAN STIR-FRY WITH BROCCOLI AND PEAS

SERVINGS	PREPARATION TIME	COOKING TIME
2	20 Mins	10 Mins

Ingredients

- ·1/4 cup (60ml) low-sodium vegetable broth
- ·1 tbsp (15ml) rice wine vinegar
- ·½ tbsp (5g) grated peeled ginger root
- ·½ tbsp (8g) cornstarch
- ·1 clove of garlic, minced
- ·½ tsp (3ml) low-sodium soy sauce
- ·½ tbsp (8ml) olive oil
- ·Half (4-oz) (110g) package seitan, cut into 2-inch (5cm) strips
- ·1 1/2 cups (180g) broccoli florets
- ·1 stalk of lemongrass, peeled and chopped
- ·1 cup (160g) snow pea pods
- ·1 cup (160g) frozen baby peas

Directions

1.Mix the broth, vinegar, ginger root, cornstarch, garlic, and soy sauce in a small bowl. Set aside.

2.Heat your large nonstick skillet or wok over medium heat. Add the olive oil. Add the seitan to the skillet and stir-fry for 2 minutes.

3.Add the broccoli florets and the lemongrass—Stir-fry for 3 to 4 minutes longer.

4.Add the pea pods and frozen peas to the skillet; stir-fry for 4 to 5 minutes or until the vegetables are crisp-tender.

5.Stir the sauce and add it to your skillet. Stir-fry for 1 to 2 minutes longer or until the sauce thickens. Serve immediately.

 NUTRITIONAL VALUE

Kcal	Carbs	Protein	Total Fat	Sat. Fat	Cholesterol
346	23g	50g	6g	2g	0mg

LENTIL PILAF

SERVINGS

2

PREPARATION TIME

10 Mins

COOKING TIME

22 Mins

Ingredients

- ·1¼ cup (200g) puy lentils
- ·1/2 tbsp (8ml) olive oil
- ·Half of 1 leek, white and light green parts, rinsed & chopped
- ·4 oz (110g) (sliced cremini mushrooms
- ·1 bay leaf
- ·1 carrot, sliced
- ·3/4 cup (90g) frozen corn
- ·2 cups (475ml) low-sodium vegetable broth
- ·1 tbsp (10g) chopped fresh basil
- ·1/2 tbsp (5g) minced fresh chives

Directions

1.Sort through the lentils to remove any small stones. In a colander, rinse and drain the lentils, and set aside.

2.Heat the olive oil in your large saucepan over medium heat. Add the leeks, mushrooms, bay leaf, carrots, and corn, and cook for 2 minutes, stirring frequently.

3.Stir in the lentils and the broth and bring to a simmer. Adjust to low heat, cover the pan, and simmer within 20 minutes or until the lentils are tender.

4.Remove from the heat and discard the bay leaf. Stir in the fresh basil and chives, and serve.

 NUTRITIONAL VALUE

Kcal	Carbs	Protein	Total Fat	Sat. Fat	Cholesterol
348	59g	19g	6g	1g	0mg

THAI SOBA NOODLES WITH SPRING VEGGIES

SERVINGS
2

PREPARATION TIME
15 Mins

COOKING TIME
15 Mins

Ingredients

- ·1/4 cup (60ml) low-sodium vegetable broth
- ·½ tbsp (8g) cornstarch
- ·½ tbsp (8g) yellow curry paste
- ·½ tsp (3ml) low-sodium soy sauce
- ·⅛ tsp (0,5g) ground ginger
- ·7 oz (200g) soba noodles
- ·1 tsp (5ml) sesame oil
- ·1 1/2 green onions,
- chopped
- ·2 cloves garlic, minced
  ·1/2 cup (80g) shelled
- edamame
  ·1/2 cup (80g) baby carrots, cut in half lengthwise
  ·1 cup (160g) snow pea
- pods
  ·1 cup (90g) asparagus cut into 1-inch (2,5cm) pieces;
- woody ends trimmed
  ·1 tbsp (10g) chopped fresh chives

Directions

1.Boil a large pot of water.

2.Meanwhile, in your small bowl, whisk together the broth, cornstarch, curry paste, soy sauce, and ginger, and set aside.

3.Cook your soba noodles according to package instructions until al dente. Drain, rinse, and set aside.

4.Heat the sesame oil in a large nonstick skillet or wok over medium-high heat. Add the green onions and garlic, and stir-fry for 2 minutes.

5.Add the edamame and baby carrots, and stir-fry for 3 minutes. Add the snow pea pods and asparagus, and stir-fry for 3 minutes.

6.Add the noodles and the sauce, and stir-fry for 2 to 3 minutes or until the sauce thickens. Sprinkle with the chives, and serve immediately.

 NUTRITIONAL VALUE

Kcal	Carbs	Protein	Total Fat	Sat. Fat	Cholesterol
379	68g	18g	7g	1g	0mg

VEGAN RATATOUILLE

SERVINGS

2

PREPARATION TIME

10 Mins

COOKING TIME

10-15 Mins

Ingredients

- ·½ tbsp (8ml) olive oil
- ·1 onion, chopped
- ·2 cloves garlic, minced
- ·Half of 1 red bell pepper, seeded and chopped
- ·Half of 1 small aubergine, diced
- ·Half of 1 yellow summer squash, diced
- ·1 (14-oz) (400g) can of no-salt-added diced tomatoes
- ·1 ½ tbsp (25g) (no-salt-added tomato paste
- ·Pinch of salt
- ·½ tsp (2g) dried Italian seasoning
- ·Half of 1 (8-oz) (220g) can of no-salt-added cannellini beans, rinsed and drained
- ·1 tbsp (3g) minced fresh basil
- ·1 tbsp (5g) pitted and sliced black olives

Directions

1.Heat a large skillet over medium heat. Add the olive oil, onion, garlic, bell pepper, aubergine, and summer squash.

2.Stir the vegetables, then add the tomatoes, tomato paste, salt, and Italian seasoning. Stir in the beans.

3.Simmer over medium heat for 10 to 15 minutes, frequently stirring, until the vegetables are tender. Sprinkle with the basil and olives, and serve.

 NUTRITIONAL VALUE

Kcal	Carbs	Protein	Total Fat	Sat. Fat	Cholesterol
261	43g	12g	6g	1g	1mg

ROASTED TOFU WITH TOMATOES AND PEACHES

SERVINGS	PREPARATION TIME	COOKING TIME
2	10 Mins	18-20 Mins

Ingredients

- ·Half of 1 (8-oz) (220g) package of extra-firm tofu, drained
- ·½ tbsp (8ml) pure maple syrup
- ·½ tsp (3ml) sesame oil
- ·½ tsp (2g) paprika
- ·1/8 tsp (0,5g) ground ginger
- ·⅛ tsp (0,5g) cayenne pepper
- ·Pinch of ground cinnamon & salt
- ·1 cup (125g) yellow or red cherry tomatoes
- ·1/2 cup (60g) grape tomatoes
- ·2 peaches, peeled and sliced
- ·1 tbsp (15ml) fresh lemon juice

Directions

1.Preheat the oven to 425°F (220°C). Line your baking sheet using aluminum foil and set aside.

2.Press the tofu between sheets of paper towel to remove excess moisture. Cut the tofu into 2 slices. Place on the prepared baking sheet.

3.In a small bowl, combine the maple syrup, sesame oil, paprika, ginger, cayenne pepper, and cinnamon. Brush onto the tofu slices.

4.Surround the tofu with tomatoes and peaches. Sprinkle the fruit with lemon juice and salt.

5.Roast for 18 to 20 minutes or until the tofu is lightly browned and the fruit is soft. Serve the tofu topped with the fruit mixture.

 NUTRITIONAL VALUE

Kcal	Carbs	Protein	Total Fat	Sat. Fat	Cholesterol
198	23g	13g	8g	1g	0mg

LENTIL BOLOGNESE

SERVINGS
2

PREPARATION TIME
10 Mins

COOKING TIME
30 Mins

Ingredients

- ·1/2 cup (80g) red lentils
- ·1 tsp (5ml) olive oil
- ·1 onion, chopped
- ·1/2 cup (30g) sliced mushrooms
- ·1 clove of garlic, minced
- ·1 small carrot, grated
- ·1/2 tsp (3g) dried Italian seasoning
- ·1 ½ cups (350ml) low-sodium vegetable broth
- ·1/4 cup (60ml) dry red wine (optional)
- ·4 oz (110g) brown rice pasta or quinoa spaghetti
- ·Half of 1 (7-ounce) (200g) can of no-salt-added diced tomatoes, drained
- ·Half of 1 1 (4-ounce) (110g) can of no-salt-added tomato sauce
- ·1 tbsp (3g) chopped fresh basil

Directions

1.Sort the lentils and rinse them, then set them aside.
2.Heat the olive oil in your large skillet over medium-high heat. Add the onion, mushrooms, and garlic, then cook for 2 minutes, stirring frequently.
3.Add the carrot, Italian seasoning, lentils, vegetable broth, and red wine (if using), and bring to a simmer.
4.Adjust to low heat and cook for 18 to 20 minutes, partially covered and often stirring, until the lentils are soft.
5.Meanwhile, boil a large pot of water, add your pasta, and cook until al dente. Drain and set aside.
6.When the lentils are soft, add the tomatoes and the tomato sauce and simmer for 2 to 3 minutes. Serve the lentil sauce over the cooked spaghetti, topped with fresh basil.

 NUTRITIONAL VALUE

Kcal	Carbs	Protein	Total Fat	Sat. Fat	Cholesterol
429	79g	18g	4g	1g	1mg

SPICY PINTO BEAN QUINOA BOWL

SERVINGS	PREPARATION TIME	COOKING TIME
2	15 Mins	35 Mins

Ingredients

- ·1/4 cup (50g) quinoa
- ·3/4 cup (180ml) low-sodium vegetable broth
- ·Pinch of salt
- ·⅛ teaspoon (1g) white pepper
- ·½ tsp (3ml) olive oil
- ·1 onion, chopped
- ·2 cloves garlic, minced
- ·Half of 1 jalapeño pepper, seeded & minced
- ·Half of 1 (8-oz) (220g) can of no-salt-added pinto beans, rinsed & drained
- ·1/4 cup (50ml) low-sodium salsa
- ·1/4 cup (50ml) low-sodium tomato sauce
- ·1 tsp (5g) chili powder
- ·1 tbsp (15ml) orange juice
- ·Half of 1 avocado, rinsed, peeled, & chopped
- ·1/4 cup (5g) chopped fresh flat-leaf parsley

Directions

1.Place the quinoa in a fine-mesh strainer. Run under cool water until the water runs clear.

2.In your medium saucepan over medium heat, combine the quinoa, broth, and salt and bring to a simmer.

3.Simmer for 20 minutes or until the quinoa is soft and fluffy. Remove from the heat.

4.Meanwhile, heat the olive oil in your large nonstick skillet over medium heat. Add the onion, garlic, and jalapeño pepper, then sauté for 3 to 4 minutes.

5.Add the pinto beans, salsa, tomato sauce, and chili powder, and bring to a simmer. Simmer, frequently stirring, until the vegetables are tender.

6.Stir the orange juice into the quinoa, and then spoon it into bowls. Top with the bean mixture, avocado, and parsley, and serve immediately.

 NUTRITIONAL VALUE

Kcal	Carbs	Protein	Total Fat	Sat. Fat	Cholesterol
446	69g	20g	12g	2g	0mg

BUTTERNUT SQUASH, BULGUR, AND TEMPEH BURRITOS

SERVINGS
2

PREPARATION TIME
15 Mins

COOKING TIME
35 Mins

Ingredients

- ·1 tsp (5ml) olive oil
- ·1 cup (120g) chopped butternut squash
- ·½ cup (40g) chopped onion
- ·½ cup (50g) cooked bulgur
- ·½ cup (50g) crumbled tempeh
- ·½ tsp (3g) chili powder
- ·¼ tsp (2g) ground cumin
- ·4 (6-inch) (15cm) whole-grain tortillas
- ·½ cup (120ml) low-sodium tomato or mango salsa
- ·1 scallion, white and green parts, sliced
- ·½ cup (15g) shredded lettuce
- ·¼ cup (60ml) fat-free sour cream

Directions

1.In a medium skillet, warm the olive oil over medium-high heat. Add the squash and onions, then sauté for 8 to 10 minutes until tender.

2.Add the bulgur, tempeh, chili powder, and cumin, then sauté for 7 minutes until the bulgur is heated through.

3.Wrap the tortillas in your clean kitchen towel and heat in your microwave for 15 to 30 seconds.

4.Lay the tortillas out and evenly divide the squash mixture between them. Top each with salsa, scallion, lettuce, and sour cream. Wrap the tortillas around your filling and serve.

 NUTRITIONAL VALUE

Kcal	Carbs	Protein	Total Fat	Sat. Fat	Cholesterol
423	64g	19g	13g	2g	4mg

CAULIFLOWER WITH ORZO AND BLACK BEANS

SERVINGS	PREPARATION TIME	COOKING TIME
2	10 Mins	16-18 Mins

Ingredients

- ·1 tsp (5ml) olive oil
- ·1 1/2 cups (180g) fresh cauliflower florets in bite-sized pieces
- ·1 clove of garlic, minced
- ·Half of 1 yellow bell pepper, seeded & chopped into bite-sized pieces
- ·Half of 1 (8-oz) (220g) can of no-salt-added black beans, rinsed & drained
- ·1 1/2 cups (350ml) low-sodium vegetable broth
- ·3/4 cups (120g) orzo
- ·½ tsp (1g) dried thyme leaves
- ·Pinch of salt
- ·⅛ tsp (1g) white pepper
- ·Half of 1 (7-oz) (200g) can of no-salt-added diced tomatoes, undrained
- ·1 cup (20g) baby spinach leaves
- ·1 tbsp (10g) grated Romano cheese

Directions

1. Heat the olive oil in your large nonstick skillet over medium heat. Add the cauliflower and garlic and sauté for 6 minutes, often stirring, until the cauliflower is lightly browned. Add the bell pepper and stir well.
2. Add the beans, broth, orzo, thyme, salt, and white pepper. Stir and bring to a simmer.
3. Adjust to low heat and simmer for 8 to 10 minutes or until the orzo is cooked.
4. Add the tomatoes, and simmer for 1 minute longer. Stir in the spinach; remove the pan, cover it, and let it stand for 1 minute.
5. Remove the cover, sprinkle with the cheese, and serve immediately.

 NUTRITIONAL VALUE

Kcal	Carbs	Protein	Total Fat	Sat. Fat	Cholesterol
435	19g	5g	5g	1g	4mg

TOFU AND ROOT VEGETABLE CURRY

SERVINGS
2

PREPARATION TIME
15 Mins

COOKING TIME
25 Mins

Ingredients

- ·2 tsp (10ml) olive oil
- ·1 cup (100g) small cauliflower florets
- ·1 parsnip, diced
- ·1 carrot, diced
- ·1 red bell pepper, thinly sliced
- ·1 cup (100g) diced sweet potato
- ·1 tsp (3g) peeled, grated fresh ginger
- ·½ tsp (2g) minced garlic
- ·1 cup (240ml) low-sodium vegetable broth
- ·2 tomatoes, chopped
- ·2 cups (150g) diced extra-firm tofu
- ·2 tbsp (15g) curry powder or paste
- ·¼ cup (30g)chopped cashews, for garnish

Directions

1.In your large saucepan, warm the olive oil over medium-high heat.

2.Add the cauliflower, parsnips, carrots, bell peppers, sweet potatoes, ginger, and garlic, then sauté for 10 minutes until the vegetables soften.

3.Stir in the vegetable broth, tomatoes, tofu, and curry powder, and bring the mixture to a boil.

4.Adjust to low heat and simmer for 15 to 18 minutes until the vegetables are tender and everything is completely heated through. Serve topped with cashews.

 NUTRITIONAL VALUE

Kcal	Carbs	Protein	Total Fat	Sat. Fat	Cholesterol
457	60g	19g	2g	3g	0mg

SOUTHWESTERN MILLET-STUFFED TOMATOES

SERVINGS

2

PREPARATION TIME

15 Mins

COOKING TIME

25 Mins

Ingredients

- ·4 large tomatoes
- ·¼ tsp (2g) sea salt
- ·2 tsp (10ml) olive oil
- ·1 sweet onion, chopped
- ·1 orange bell pepper, chopped
- ·2 small courgette
- ·½ jalapeño pepper, finely chopped
- ·1 tsp (3g) minced garlic
- ·2 cups (100g) cooked millet
- ·1 cup (90g) fresh or frozen corn kernels (thawed, if frozen)
- ·Juice of ½ lime
- ·¼ cup (25g) grated Parmesan cheese
- ·2 tsp (5g) chopped fresh coriander for garnish

Directions

1.Preheat the oven to 350°F (180°C).

2.Cut the tops off the tomatoes and discard. Carefully scoop out the insides of the tomatoes, leaving the shells intact.

3.Sprinkle the inside of the tomatoes with salt and turn them upside down on paper towels to drain for about 15 minutes.

4.Meanwhile, warm the olive oil in a large skillet over medium-high heat. Add the onions, bell peppers, courgette, jalapeño, and garlic, and sauté for 5 minutes until softening.

5.Stir in the millet, corn, and lime juice, then sauté for 5 to 6 minutes until warm. Place the tomatoes, hollow-side up, in a medium baking dish.

6.Divide the millet mixture evenly among the tomatoes and top with the Parmesan cheese. Bake for 15 minutes or until the filling is completely heated through. Serve topped with coriander.

 NUTRITIONAL VALUE

Kcal	Carbs	Protein	Total Fat	Sat. Fat	Cholesterol
464	80g	16g	10g	2g	10mg

CHILI-SAUTÉED TOFU WITH ALMONDS

SERVINGS
2

PREPARATION TIME
20 Mins

COOKING TIME
15 Mins

Ingredients

- ·2 tsp (10ml) olive oil
- ·½ jalapeño pepper, chopped
- ·1 tsp (3g) grated fresh ginger
- ·1 tsp (3g) minced garlic
- ·12 oz (340g) extra-firm tofu, drained and cut into 1-inch (2,5cm) cubes
- ·2 cups (60g) shredded bok choy
- ·1 red bell pepper, thinly sliced
- ·1 scallion, white & green parts, thinly sliced
- ·1 tbsp (15ml) low-sodium tamari sauce
- ·1 tbsp (15ml) freshly squeezed lime juice
- ·1 cup (90g) cooked quinoa for serving
- ·¼ cup (30g) chopped almonds, for garnish

Directions

1.In your large skillet, warm the olive oil over medium-high heat. Add the jalapeño, ginger, and garlic, then sauté for 4 minutes until softened.
2.Add the tofu, bok choy, bell peppers, and green onions, then sauté for 8 to 10 minutes until the tofu is lightly browned and the vegetables are tender. 3.Stir in the tamari sauce and lime juice and toss to coat the ingredients. Serve over quinoa, topped with chopped almonds.

 NUTRITIONAL VALUE

Kcal	Carbs	Protein	Total Fat	Sat. Fat	Cholesterol
469	43g	28g	24g	2g	0mg

BROWN RICE AND SWEET POTATO PILAF

SERVINGS
2

PREPARATION TIME
10 Mins

COOKING TIME
1 hour & 5 Mins

Ingredients

- ·1 tsp (5ml) olive oil
- ·½ cup (40g) chopped sweet onion
- ·1 tsp (3g) minced garlic
- ·½ cup (80g) brown rice
- ·1½ cups (350ml) low-sodium vegetable broth
- ·⅛ tsp (1g) ground cumin
- ·½ sweet potato, peeled and cut into ¼-inch (0,5cm) cubes
- ·½ cup (80g) low-sodium canned haricot beans, rinsed & drained
- ·1 cup (20g) fresh baby spinach
- ·1 tsp (5g) plant-sterol margarine
- ·Sea salt & ground black pepper
- ·2 tbsp (20g) chopped cashews, for garnish
- ·1 tsp (3g) chopped fresh parsley, for garnish

Directions

1.In a medium saucepan, warm the olive oil over medium-high heat. Add the onions and garlic and sauté for 3 minutes until softened. Stir in the rice and sauté for 2 more minutes.

2.Stir in the broth and cumin, and bring the mixture to a boil. Reduce the heat and simmer within 25 minutes, partially covered.

3.Stir in the sweet potato and continue cooking for 25 minutes until the rice and potato are tender.

4.Stir in the beans, spinach, and margarine, and remove the pan from the heat. Let the pilaf stand for 5 minutes to allow the greens to wilt.

5.Season with salt and pepper. Serve topped with cashews and parsley.

 NUTRITIONAL VALUE

Kcal	Carbs	Protein	Total Fat	Sat. Fat	Cholesterol
390	68g	12g	8g	1g	0mg

SOUPS & STEWS

MINESTRONE FLORENTINE SOUP

SERVINGS

2

PREPARATION TIME

10 Mins

COOKING TIME

25 Mins

Ingredients

- ·1 tsp (5ml) olive oil
- ·1 beetrootss stalk, diced
- ·1 carrot, thinly sliced
- ·¼ sweet onion, peeled and chopped
- ·1 tsp (3g) minced garlic
- ·3 cups (700ml) low-sodium vegetable broth
- ·1 cup (150g) low-sodium canned diced tomatoes, with their juices
- ·1 cup (150g) low-sodium canned cannellini beans, rinsed and drained
- ·1 cup (20g) fresh baby spinach
- ·1 tsp (3g) chopped fresh basil
- ·Pinch of red pepper flakes
- ·Sea salt & ground black pepper to taste

Directions

1.In a medium saucepan, warm the olive oil over medium-high heat. Add the beetrootss, carrots, onions, and garlic, then sauté for 5 minutes until softened. 2.Stir in the vegetable broth, tomatoes, and beans, and bring the soup to a boil. Adjust to low heat and simmer for 15 minutes until the vegetables are tender.

3.Remove the soup and stir in the spinach, basil, and red pepper flakes. Let it stand for 5 minutes to allow the spinach to wilt. Season with salt and pepper and serve.

 NUTRITIONAL VALUE

Kcal	Carbs	Protein	Total Fat	Sat. Fat	Cholesterol
190	30g	10g	3g	0g	0mg

FALL VEGETABLES CHICKEN SOUP

SERVINGS

2

PREPARATION TIME

10 Mins

COOKING TIME

20-35 Mins

Ingredients

- ·1 tsp (5ml) olive oil
- ·2 beetrootss stalks, thinly sliced ·2 carrots, diced
- ·2 parsnips, diced
- ·¼ sweet onion, peeled and chopped
- ·1 tsp (3g) minced garlic
- ·4 cups (900ml) low-sodium chicken broth
- ·1 cup (90g) diced sweet potato
- ·1 cup (90g) diced cooked chicken breast
- ·½ tsp (1g) chopped fresh thyme
- ·1 cup (90) small broccoli florets
- ·Sea salt & ground black pepper to taste

Directions

1.In a medium saucepan, warm the oil over medium-high heat. Add the beetrootss, carrots, parsnips, onions, and garlic, then sauté for 7 to 8 minutes until softened.

2.Stir in the broth, sweet potato, chicken, and thyme, and bring the soup to a boil. Adjust to low heat and simmer for 20 minutes.

3.Add the broccoli and simmer for 5 minutes until all the vegetables are tender. Season with salt and pepper and serve.

 NUTRITIONAL VALUE

Kcal	Carbs	Protein	Total Fat	Sat. Fat	Cholesterol
309	40g	26g	3g	0g	0mg

VEGETABLE AND BARLEY SOUP

SERVINGS	PREPARATION TIME	COOKING TIME
2	10 Mins	1 hour & 4 Mins

Ingredients

- ·1 tsp (5ml) olive oil
- ·1 beetrootss stalk,
- chopped
  ·¼ sweet onion, peeled and
- chopped
- ·½ tsp (3g) minced garlic
  ·5 cups (1,2l) low-sodium
- vegetable broth
- ·½ cup (90g) hulled barley
- ·1 carrot, thinly sliced
  ·½ cup (45g) small broccoli
- florets
- ·½ red bell pepper, diced
  ·½ cup (50g) green beans,
  trimmed & cut into 1-inch
- pieces
  ·½ cup (45g) small
- cauliflower florets
  ·½ cup (15g) shredded red
- cabbage
  ·Sea salt & ground black
- pepper
  ·2 tsp (5g) chopped fresh
  parsley, for garnish

Directions

1.In a medium saucepan, warm the olive oil over medium-high heat. Add the beetrootss, onions, and garlic, then sauté for 4 minutes until softened.

2.Stir in the vegetable broth and barley and bring to a boil. Adjust to low heat and simmer for 40 minutes.

3.Stir in the carrots, broccoli, bell peppers, green beans, cauliflower, and cabbage, and simmer for 20 minutes until the vegetables and barley are tender.

4.Season the soup with salt and pepper. Serve topped with parsley.

 NUTRITIONAL VALUE

Kcal	Carbs	Protein	Total Fat	Sat. Fat	Cholesterol
219	40g	10g	4g	0g	0mg

CHICKEN ALPHABET SOUP

SERVINGS
2

PREPARATION TIME
15 Mins

COOKING TIME
20 Mins

Ingredients

- ·1 tsp (5ml) olive oil
- ·2 beetrootss stalks, thinly
- sliced ·½ small sweet onion, peeled and
- chopped
- ·½ tsp (3g) minced garlic ·4 cups (900ml) low-
- sodium chicken broth
- ·2 carrots, diced ·1 cup (90g) diced cooked
- chicken breast ·½ cup (50g) dry alphabet
- pasta ·1 tsp (2g) chopped fresh
- thyme ·½ cup (10g) shredded
- Swiss chard ·Freshly ground black pepper to taste

Directions

1.In a medium saucepan, warm the olive oil over medium-high heat. Add the beetrootss, onions, and garlic, then sauté for 4 minutes until softened.
2.Stir in the broth, carrots, chicken, pasta, and thyme. Let it boil, adjust to low heat, and simmer the soup for 15 minutes until the noodles are cooked through.
3.Stir in the chard and season the soup with pepper. Serve.

 NUTRITIONAL VALUE

Kcal	Carbs	Protein	Total Fat	Sat. Fat	Cholesterol
233	22g	25g	5g	1g	54mg

CURRIED CAULIFLOWER-LENTIL SOUP

SERVINGS	PREPARATION TIME	COOKING TIME
2	10 Mins	25 Mins

Ingredients

- ·1 tsp (5ml) olive oil
- ·½ cup (40g) chopped sweet onion
- ·1 tsp (3g) minced garlic
- ·1 tsp (2g) peeled, grated fresh ginger
- ·1 small head of cauliflower, roughly chopped
- ·1 cup (90g) low-sodium canned lentils, rinsed and drained
- ·4 cups (900ml) low-sodium vegetable broth
- ·1 tbsp (10g) curry powder
- ·Sea salt to taste
- ·¼ cup (60g) low-fat plain kefir
- ·1 tsp (3g) chopped fresh coriander, for garnish

Directions

1.In your large saucepan, warm the olive oil over medium-high heat. Add the onion, garlic, and ginger, then sauté for 3 minutes until softened.

2.Stir in the cauliflower, lentils, broth, and curry powder, and bring the mixture to a boil. Adjust to low heat and simmer for 20 minutes until the cauliflower is tender.

3.Transfer the soup to a food processor and process until smooth. Return the soup to the saucepan or a bowl and stir in the kefir. Serve topped with coriander.

 NUTRITIONAL VALUE

Kcal	Carbs	Protein	Total Fat	Sat. Fat	Cholesterol
231	37g	17g	3g	0g	3mg

SAUSAGE WHITE BEAN STEW

SERVINGS
2

PREPARATION TIME
10 Mins

COOKING TIME
22 Mins

Ingredients

- ·14 oz (400g) canned diced tomatoes, no-salt-added
- ·4 oz (110g) sweet Italian turkey sausage, casings removed
- ·1 1/2 (30g) cup baby spinach
- ·1/4 (20g) cup chopped white onion
- ·7 oz (200g) canned cannellini beans, drained & rinsed
- ·¼ tsp (1g) ground black pepper
- ·½ tbsp (8ml) olive oil
- ·1/2 cup (120ml) water

Directions

1.Heat a large saucepan with the oil over medium heat. Add the onion and sausage, then cook for 6 minutes.

2.Add the beans, tomatoes, water, and black pepper, then cook for 15 minutes. Add the spinach, and cook for 1 minute until the spinach leaves wilt. Serve.

 NUTRITIONAL VALUE

Kcal	Carbs	Protein	Total Fat	Sat. Fat	Cholesterol
254	27g	16g	8g	1g	47mg

TUSCAN FISH STEW

SERVINGS	PREPARATION TIME	COOKING TIME
2	10 Mins	20 Mins

Ingredients

- ·½ tbsp (8ml) olive oil
- ·1/2 onion, chopped
- ·1 clove of garlic, minced
- ·1 1/2 large tomatoes, chopped
- ·1/2 bulb fennel, peeled, chopped, and rinsed
- ·7 oz (200g) canned artichoke hearts, drained
- ·1 bay leaf
- ·⅛ tsp (1g) red pepper flakes
- ·1 cup (240ml) low-sodium vegetable broth
- ·1/2-pound (220g) halibut fillets, cubed
- ·1/8-pound (30g) sea scallops
- ·1 slice of low-sodium whole-wheat bread, crumbled
- ·1 tbsp (3g) chopped fresh basil
- ·1 tsp (3g) chopped fresh oregano
- ·1 tbsp (3g) chopped fresh flat-leaf parsley

Directions

1.Heat the olive oil in your stockpot or large saucepan over medium heat. Add the onion and garlic, then cook while stirring within 3 minutes.

2.Add the tomatoes, fennel, artichoke hearts, bay leaf, red pepper flakes, and vegetable broth, and bring to a simmer. Simmer for 5 minutes.

3.Add the halibut fillets, and simmer for 4 minutes. Add the scallops, and simmer for 3 minutes, or until the fillets flake when tested with a fork and the scallops are opaque.

4.Stir in the bread crumbs, then cover the pan and remove from the heat. Let it stand for 3 minutes.

5.Remove and discard the bay leaf. Top the soup with fresh basil, oregano, and parsley, and serve.

 NUTRITIONAL VALUE

Kcal	Carbs	Protein	Total Fat	Sat. Fat	Cholesterol
210	28g	29g	6g	1g	9mg

BABA GHANOUSH STEW

SERVINGS
2

PREPARATION TIME
15 Mins

COOKING TIME
42 Mins

Ingredients

- ·2 small aubergines, cut in half and scored with a crosshatch pattern on the cut sides
- ·2 tsp (10ml) olive oil
- ·1 cup (90g) chopped fennel
- ·½ cup (40g) chopped sweet onion
- ·1 tsp (3g) minced garlic
- ·½ tsp (2g) ground cumin
- ·¼ tsp (1g) ground coriander
- ·4 cups (1l) low-sodium vegetable broth
- ·2 tbsp (30g) tahini
- ·Juice of ½ lemon
- ·2 tomatoes, chopped
- ·Sea salt & ground black pepper
- ·1 tsp (3g) chopped fresh parsley, for garnish

Directions

1.Preheat the oven to 400°F (200°C). Line your baking sheet using parchment paper and place the aubergine, cut side down, on the sheet.

2.Roast the aubergine for 20 to 25 minutes until soft. Remove and set aside to cool slightly for 10 minutes.

3.In your large saucepan, warm the olive oil over medium-high heat. Add the fennel, onion, garlic, cumin, and coriander, then sauté for 6 to 7 minutes until softened.

4.Discarding the skin, place the roasted aubergine into a blender or food processor. Add the vegetable broth, tahini, and lemon juice, then purée until smooth.

5.Add the puréed aubergine to the saucepan and stir in the tomatoes. Let it boil, adjust to low heat, and simmer for 10 minutes—season with salt and pepper. Serve topped with parsley.

 NUTRITIONAL VALUE

Kcal	Carbs	Protein	Total Fat	Sat. Fat	Cholesterol
338	49g	11g	14g	2g	0mg

HEARTY VEGETABLE STEW

SERVINGS	PREPARATION TIME	COOKING TIME
2	15 Mins	25 Mins

Ingredients

- ·2 tsp (10ml) olive oil
- ·2 beetrootss stalks, chopped
- ·½ sweet onion, peeled and chopped
- ·1 tsp (3g) minced garlic
- ·3 cups (700ml) low-sodium vegetable broth
- ·1 cup (90g) chopped tomatoes
- ·2 carrots, thinly sliced
- ·1 cup (90g) cauliflower florets
- ·1 cup (90g) broccoli florets
- ·1 yellow bell pepper, diced
- ·1 cup (100g) low-sodium canned black beans, rinsed & drained
- ·Pinch red pepper flakes
- ·Sea salt & ground black pepper to taste
- ·2 tbsp (30g) grated low-fat Parmesan cheese for garnish
- ·1 tbsp (10g) chopped fresh parsley, for garnish

Directions

1.In your large saucepan, warm the olive oil over medium-high heat. Add the beetrootss, onions, and garlic, then sauté for 4 minutes until softened.

2.Stir in the vegetable broth, tomatoes, carrots, cauliflower, broccoli, bell peppers, black beans, and red pepper flakes.

3.Bring the stew to a boil, then reduce the heat to low and simmer for 18 to 20 minutes until the vegetables are tender.

4.Season with salt and pepper. Serve topped with Parmesan cheese and parsley.

 NUTRITIONAL VALUE

Kcal	Carbs	Protein	Total Fat	Sat. Fat	Cholesterol
270	35g	17g	8g	3g	10mg

CURRIED CHICKPEA STEW

SERVINGS	PREPARATION TIME	COOKING TIME
2	20 Mins	40-45 Mins

Ingredients

- ·7 oz (200g) canned chickpeas, drained, & rinsed
- ·3/4 cup (60g) cauliflower florets
- ·1 small white onion, peeled, & chopped
- ·3 oz (85g) spinach leaves
- ·7 oz (200g) no-salt-added canned diced tomatoes, drained
- ·1 small carrot, peeled, & sliced
- ·½ tsp (2g) garlic, minced
- ·1 small jalapeño pepper, deseeded, & chopped
- ·1 (1 inch) (2,5cm) piece of ginger, peeled, & minced
- ·¼ tbsp (1g) curry powder
- ·½ tbsp (8ml) **sunflower**
- oil
  ·1 ½ tbsp (20ml) nonfat
- unsweetened coconut milk
  ·1/8 cup (30ml) fat-free half cream

Directions

1.Place the spinach leaves in your heatproof dish, drizzle with 1 tbsp water, cover the bowl with plastic wrap, and microwave at a high heat setting for 1 to 2 minutes.

2.Transfer the spinach to a colander, drain it well and let it cool slightly. Squeeze the spinach to drain excess moisture, chop it finely and set it aside.

3.Heat a large skillet pan with oil over medium heat. Add the onion and cook for 8 minutes until softened.

4.Add the garlic, ginger, jalapeno pepper, and curry powder, and continue cooking for 30 seconds until fragrant.

5.Add the carrots, and 2 tbsp of water, then cover and cook for 10 minutes until softened. Stir in the cauliflower, cover the pan again and cook for 5 to 10 minutes until florets turn tender-crisp.

6.Add the tomatoes, chickpeas, coconut milk, and half cream, then bring the mixture to a boil.

7.Adjust to low heat, uncover the pan and cook for 15 minutes.

8.Add the chopped spinach, stir well and cook for 1 minute until thoroughly hot. Let the stew cool for 5 minutes, and serve.

 NUTRITIONAL VALUE

Kcal	Carbs	Protein	Total Fat	Sat. Fat	Cholesterol
241	39g	11g	6g	0g	0mg

MEAT

MAPLE-BALSAMIC PORK CHOPS

SERVINGS
2

PREPARATION TIME
10 Mins

COOKING TIME
20 Mins

Ingredients

- ·2 (4-oz) (110g) boneless pork top-loin chops
- ·¼ cup (60ml) low-sodium chicken broth
- ·2 tbsp (30ml) maple syrup
- ·1 tbsp (15ml) balsamic vinegar
- ·¼ tsp (1g) chopped fresh thyme
- ·Sea salt & ground black pepper to taste
- ·Nonstick olive oil cooking spray

Directions

1.In a small bowl, stir together the chicken broth, maple syrup, vinegar, and thyme. Flavor your pork chops on both sides with sea salt and pepper.

2.Place your medium skillet over medium-high heat and spray generously with cooking spray. Add the pork chops and cook within 6 minutes on each side.

3.Add the sauce to the skillet and turn the chops to coat thoroughly. Continue to cook within 6 minutes more until the pork chops are cooked through, turning once.

4.Let the pork rest for 10 minutes and serve.

 NUTRITIONAL VALUE

Kcal	Carbs	Protein	Total Fat	Sat. Fat	Cholesterol
153	14g	24g	7g	2g	65mg

LEMON BASIL PORK MEDALLIONS

SERVINGS
2

PREPARATION TIME
15 Mins

COOKING TIME
6 Mins

Ingredients

- ·1/2-pound (220g) plain pork tenderloin, sliced crosswise into 1-inch slices
- ·1/4 (1g) tsp dried basil leaves
- ·⅛ tsp (0,5g) lemon pepper
- ·1 1/2 (13g) tablespoons cornstarch
- ·1/2 tsp (2ml) olive oil
- ·2 cloves of garlic, minced
- ·1/2 cup (120ml) chicken broth
- ·1 ½ tbsp (20ml) fresh lemon juice
- ·1 tsp (3g) fresh lemon zest
- ·1 1/2 (6g) tbsp chopped fresh basil
- ·Pinch of salt

Directions

1.Place the slices on a piece of plastic wrap or parchment paper. Cover with another piece of plastic wrap. Put on a cutting board.

2.Using a rolling pin or meat mallet, gently pound the slices until they are about ½-inch thick.

3.Combine the dried basil, salt, lemon pepper, and cornstarch on a plate. Add the tenderloin slices and toss to coat.

4.Heat your large nonstick skillet over medium heat and add the olive oil. Add half the tenderloin slices and cook for 2 minutes until browned.

5.Turn the pork and cook on the other side for 1 to 2 minutes. Remove from the skillet to a clean plate. Repeat with remaining pork.

6.Add the garlic to your pan and cook for 1 minute, stirring constantly. Add the chicken broth, lemon juice, and lemon zest, and bring to a simmer.

7.Put the pork slices back in the skillet, and simmer within 2 to 3 minutes until sauce thickens slightly. Stir in the fresh basil leaves, and serve.

 NUTRITIONAL VALUE

Kcal	Carbs	Protein	Total Fat	Sat. Fat	Cholesterol
170	8g	21g	6g	2g	50mg

EASY PORK BURGERS

SERVINGS
2

PREPARATION TIME
15 Mins

COOKING TIME
15 Mins

Ingredients

- ·½ pound (220g) extra-lean ground pork
- ·1 large egg white
- ·1 scallion, white parts only, chopped
- ·¼ cup (30g) ground almonds
- ·¼ tsp (1g) minced garlic
- ·⅛ tsp (0,5) allspice
- ·Sea salt & ground black pepper to taste

Directions

1.Preheat a grill to medium-high heat.

2.Thoroughly mix the pork, egg white, scallion, almonds, garlic, and allspice in your medium bowl. Season the mixture with salt and pepper. Form the mixture into 2 burgers.

3.Place the burgers on your grill and cook for 7 to 8 minutes per side until they are just cooked through. Serve with your favorite toppings.

 NUTRITIONAL VALUE

Kcal	Carbs	Protein	Total Fat	Sat. Fat	Cholesterol
243	4g	28g	13g	3g	55mg

HONEYED PORK TENDERLOIN WITH BUTTERNUT SQUASH

SERVINGS	PREPARATION TIME	COOKING TIME
2	15 Mins	30-35 Mins

Ingredients

- ·1 (8-oz) (220g) pork tenderloin, fat trimmed
- ·4 cups (30g) diced butternut squash
- ·1 tbsp (15ml) honey
- ·Dash of ground cloves
- ·2 tsp (10ml) sunflower oil divided
- ·¼ tsp (1g) chopped fresh thyme
- ·Sea salt & ground black pepper to taste
- ·Nonstick olive oil cooking spray

Directions

1.Preheat the oven to 425°F (220°C). Line your baking sheet using foil and lightly spray it with cooking spray.

2.Lightly season your pork with salt and pepper and rub the meat with honey. Sprinkle with cloves.

3.Heat 1 teaspoon of sunflower oil in a small skillet and brown the tenderloin on all sides for 5 minutes. Place the tenderloin on the baking sheet.

4.In a medium bowl, toss the butternut squash, remaining 1 teaspoon of sunflower oil, and thyme until well mixed.

5.Spread the squash around the tenderloin and lightly season the vegetables with salt and pepper.

6.Place the baking sheet in your oven and roast within 25 to 30 minutes until the meat is cooked through and the squash is tender. Serve.

 NUTRITIONAL VALUE

Kcal	Carbs	Protein	Total Fat	Sat. Fat	Cholesterol
310	41g	27g	8g	1g	55mg

PORK CUTLETS WITH FENNEL AND KALE

SERVINGS
2

PREPARATION TIME
15 Mins

COOKING TIME
20 Mins

Ingredients

- ·2 (4-oz) (110g) boneless pork top-loin chops
- ·1 small fennel bulb, thinly sliced
- ·2 cups (40g) shredded kale
- ·2 tsp (10ml) olive oil, divided
- ·½ cup (40g) chopped sweet onion
- ·1 tsp (3g) garlic
- ·¼ cup (60ml) white wine
- ·¼ cup (60ml) low-sodium chicken broth
- ·Sea salt & ground black pepper to taste
- ·2 tsp (4g) chopped fresh basil for garnish

Directions

1.Pound the pork chops to about ¼-inch (0,6cm) thick between two sheets of parchment paper and season each with salt and pepper.

2.In a large skillet, heat 1 teaspoon olive oil over medium-high heat and sear the pork for 4 minutes per side until lightly browned. Remove the pork and cover with foil to keep warm.

3.Add the remaining olive oil to your skillet and sauté the fennel, onions, and garlic for 6 to 7 minutes until softened.

4.Add the wine and chicken broth to your skillet and let the liquid boil. Adjust to low heat, then simmer for 5 minutes until the liquid reduces by half.

5.Return the pork to the skillet and cook for 6 minutes until the pork is tender. Stir in the kale and simmer for 4 more minutes until the kale is wilted. Serve topped with basil.

 NUTRITIONAL VALUE

Kcal	Carbs	Protein	Total Fat	Sat. Fat	Cholesterol
366	19g	23g	20g	7g	65mg

BEEF AND BROCCOLI STIR-FRY

SERVINGS	PREPARATION TIME	COOKING TIME
2	15 Mins	6 Mins

Ingredients

- ·½ pound (220g) top sirloin steak
- ·3 cups (270g) broccoli florets
- ·3 cloves garlic, minced
- ·1 onion, chopped
- ·1¼ cups (300ml) low-sodium beef broth
- ·⅛ tsp (0.5g) cayenne pepper
- ·¼ tsp (1g) ground ginger
- ·1 tbsp (15ml) honey
- ·2 tbsp (15g) cornstarch
- ·1 tsp (6ml) hoisin sauce
- ·1 tsp (6ml) low-sodium soy sauce
- ·1 tsp (5ml) olive oil

Directions

1. Trim any visible fat from the steak. Cut the steak into ½-inch (1,2cm) strips. Place in a bowl, sprinkle with the cayenne pepper and ginger and toss. Set aside.

2. Thoroughly combine the beef broth, honey, cornstarch, hoisin sauce, and soy sauce in your small bowl. Set aside.

3. Heat the olive oil in your large nonstick skillet over medium-high heat.

4. Add the steak strips in a single layer, and cook for 1 minute. Turn the steak and cook within 1 minute longer. Transfer the steak to a plate.

5. Add the onion and garlic to the skillet, and stir-fry for 2 minutes. Add the broccoli, and stir-fry for 2 minutes.

6. Add the broth mixture and bring to a simmer. Simmer within 1 to 2 minutes or until the sauce has thickened. Return the beef to the skillet, and stir-fry for 1 minute. Serve immediately.

 NUTRITIONAL VALUE

Kcal	Carbs	Protein	Total Fat	Sat. Fat	Cholesterol
204	17g	13g	9g	3g	27mg

GRILLED COFFEE-RUBBED SIRLOIN STEAK

SERVINGS

2

PREPARATION TIME

15 Mins

COOKING TIME

14 Mins

Ingredients

- ·1 (10-oz) (280g) sirloin steak, trimmed to ⅛-inch (0,6cm) fat
- ·1 tbsp (8g) espresso coffee powder
- ·1½ tsp (7g) dark brown sugar
- ·1 tsp (5g) smoky paprika
- ·½ tsp (2g) chili powder
- ·¼ tsp (1g) each of garlic powder, ground black pepper, & salt

Directions

1. In a small bowl, stir together the espresso powder, sugar, paprika, chili powder, garlic powder, pepper, and salt. Rub the coffee mixture all over the steak.
2. Preheat the grill to medium-high. Grill the steak for 7 minutes per side, turning once, until it is the desired doneness.
3. Transfer the steak to your cutting board and let it rest for at least 10 minutes before slicing it against the grain. Serve.

 NUTRITIONAL VALUE

Kcal	Carbs	Protein	Total Fat	Sat. Fat	Cholesterol
285	4g	29g	18g	7g	67mg

DARK BEER BEEF CHILI

SERVINGS
2

PREPARATION TIME
15 Mins

COOKING TIME
39-44 Mins

Ingredients

- ·1 tsp (5ml) olive oil
- ·6 ounces (170g) of extra-lean ground beef
- ·½ sweet onion, chopped
- ·1 green bell pepper, diced
- ·1 tsp (3g) minced garlic
- ·2 cups (160g) low-sodium canned diced tomatoes, with their juices
- ·½ cup (50g) low-sodium canned kidney beans, rinsed and drained
- ·½ cup (50g) low-sodium canned lentils, rinsed and drained
- ·½ cup (120ml) dark beer
- ·1 tbsp (8g) chili powder
- ·½ tsp (2g) ground cumin
- ·Pinch of cayenne powder

Directions

1.In your large saucepan, warm the oil over medium-high heat. Add the ground beef and cook for 5 minutes until browned.

2.Add the onions, bell pepper, and garlic, then sauté for 4 minutes until softened. Stir in the tomatoes, kidney beans, lentils, beer, chili powder, cumin, and cayenne powder.

3.Let the mixture boil and then reduce the heat. Simmer for 35 to 40 minutes, partially covered, until the flavors come together and the liquid is almost gone. Serve.

 NUTRITIONAL VALUE

Kcal	Carbs	Protein	Total Fat	Sat. Fat	Cholesterol
415	49g	30g	10g	2g	63mg

SIRLOIN STEAK WITH ROOT VEGETABLES

SERVINGS
2

PREPARATION TIME
20 Mins

COOKING TIME
34-35 Mins

Ingredients

- ·1 (10-oz) (280g) sirloin steak, fat trimmed
- ·6 beetrootss, peeled & halved ·2 carrots, cut into 1-inch chunks
- ·2 parsnips, cut into 1-inch chunks
- ·1 small celeriac, peeled & cut into 1-inch chunks
- ·1 small sweet potato, peeled & cut into 1-inch chunks
- ·Sea salt & ground black pepper to taste
- ·1 tbsp (15ml) olive oil, + extra for drizzling

Directions

1.Preheat the oven to 400°F (200°C). Line a sheet pan with foil and set aside.
2.Flavor the steak with salt and pepper and set aside.
3.Spread the veggies on the sheet pan, leaving room for the steak. Season them lightly with salt and pepper and drizzle with 1 tablespoon of olive oil.
4.Roast the veggies for 30 minutes until they are lightly caramelized and tender. Remove the sheet pan and add the steak.
5.Increase the oven temperature to broil. Place your sheet pan into the oven and broil for 4 to 5 minutes per side. Serve.

 NUTRITIONAL VALUE

Kcal	Carbs	Protein	Total Fat	Sat. Fat	Cholesterol
565	51g	35g	26g	8g	67mg

BEEF BURRITO SKILLET

SERVINGS
2

PREPARATION TIME
15 Mins

COOKING TIME
13-26 Mins

Ingredients

- ·1/2-pound (220g) extra-lean ground beef
- ·1 onion, chopped
- ·2 cloves of garlic, minced
- ·1 jalapeño pepper, seeded and minced
- ·1/2 tbsp (4g) chili powder
- ·¼ tsp (1g) cumin
- ·8 oz (220g) canned no-salt-added pinto beans, rinsed and drained
- ·1 tomato, chopped
- ·1/2 cup (40g) frozen corn, thawed
- ·1/4 cup (60ml) low-sodium salsa
- ·2 corn tortillas, cut into 1-inch strips
- ·1 tbsp (10g) crumbled feta cheese
- ·1/8 cup (30ml) low-fat sour cream

Directions

1.In a large skillet, sauté the ground beef, onion, garlic, and jalapeño pepper for 5 to 7 minutes, stirring to break up the meat, until the beef is browned.
2.Add the chili powder and cumin, and stir well. Add the pinto beans, tomato, corn, and salsa, then b simmer for 5 minutes, stirring occasionally.
3.Stir in the corn tortillas and cook for 3 to 4 minutes. Top with the cheese and sour cream, and serve.

 NUTRITIONAL VALUE

Kcal	Carbs	Protein	Total Fat	Sat. Fat	Cholesterol
403	54g	32g	10g	4g	59mg

POULTRY

CHICKEN WITH MUSHROOM SAUCE

SERVINGS
2

PREPARATION TIME
10 Mins

COOKING TIME
15 Mins

Ingredients

- ·2 (6-oz) (170g) skinless, boneless chicken breasts
- ·4 oz (110g) button mushrooms, sliced
- ·1 portobello mushroom, sliced
- ·2 garlic cloves, minced
- ·¼ cup (20g) chopped shallots
- ·¼ cup (60ml) dry white wine, cooking wine, or low-sodium broth
- ·½ cup (120ml) water
- ·1 tbsp (15ml) olive oil, divided
- ·2 tsp (4g) minced fresh thyme
- ·1 tsp (6g) flour
- ·¼ tsp (1g) salt, divided
- ·⅛ tsp (0,5g) freshly ground black pepper

Directions

1.Heat 1 teaspoon of olive oil in a large nonstick skillet over medium-high heat, swirling to coat. Sprinkle the chicken with ⅛ tsp salt and pepper.
2.Add the chicken to your skillet and cook for about 3 minutes on each side. Transfer the chicken to your serving platter and keep warm.
3.Add the shallots and mushrooms to the skillet and sauté, occasionally stirring, for about 4 minutes, or until browned. Add the garlic and sauté within 1 minute, stirring constantly.
4.Add the wine and stir, scraping the pan to loosen any browned bits. Let it boil and cook until the liquid almost evaporates.
5.Sprinkle the mushroom mixture with the remaining ⅛ tsp of salt and the flour and cook for about 30 seconds, stirring constantly.
6.Add the water to the skillet and let it boil—Cook for 2 minutes more or until slightly thick.
7.Remove the skillet, add the remaining olive oil and the thyme, and stir until combined. Serve the sauce over the chicken.

 NUTRITIONAL VALUE

Kcal	Carbs	Protein	Total Fat	Sat. Fat	Cholesterol
329	12g	44g	10g	2g	97mg

BAKED CHICKEN THIGHS WITH LEAFY GREENS

SERVINGS

2

PREPARATION TIME

10 Mins

COOKING TIME

30 Mins

Ingredients

- ·2 (3-oz) (85g) boneless, skinless chicken breasts
- ·3 tsp (15ml) olive oil, divided
- ·6 cups (60g) mixed dark leafy greens (spinach, kale, Swiss chard, collard greens)
- ·1 tsp (3g) minced garlic
- ·Sea salt & ground black pepper to taste

Directions

1.Preheat the oven to 400°F (200°C). Lightly flavor the chicken breasts with salt and pepper.

2.Heat 1 teaspoon olive oil over medium-high heat in a large oven-safe skillet.

3.Add the chicken breasts and cook within 10 minutes until browned on both sides. Remove the chicken and set aside.

4.Add the remaining olive oil and sauté the greens and garlic until they are slightly wilted about 3 minutes.

5.Flavor the greens with salt and pepper and place the chicken on the greens.

6.Transfer your skillet to the oven and bake until the chicken is cooked through about 15 minutes. Serve.

 NUTRITIONAL VALUE

Kcal	Carbs	Protein	Total Fat	Sat. Fat	Cholesterol
113	4g	22g	2g	0g	49mg

HAWAIIAN CHICKEN STIR-FRY

SERVINGS
2

PREPARATION TIME
20 Mins

COOKING TIME
11 Mins

Ingredients

- ·4 oz (110g) canned crushed pineapple, undrained
- ·1/8 cup (30ml) water
- ·1 tbsp (8g) cornstarch
- ·½ tsp (3g) brown sugar
- ·½ tsp (3ml) low-sodium tamari sauce
- ·1/8 tsp (0,5g) ground ginger
- ·1/8 tsp (0,5g) cayenne pepper
- ·1 tbsp (6g) unsweetened shredded coconut
- ·1 tbsp (6g) chopped macadamia nuts
- ·½ tsp (3ml) olive oil
- ·1 onion, chopped
- ·1 red bell pepper, seeded and chopped
- ·2 (3-oz) (85g) boneless, skinless chicken breasts, cubed

Directions

1.Mix the pineapple, water, cornstarch, brown sugar, tamari, ginger, and cayenne pepper in a medium bowl. Set aside.

2.Place a large nonstick skillet or wok over medium heat. Add the coconut and macadamia nuts, and toast for 1 to 2 minutes, constantly stirring, until fragrant. Remove from the skillet and set aside.

3.Add the olive oil to your skillet and heat over medium-high heat. Add the onion and red bell pepper, then stir-fry within 2 to 3 minutes or until almost tender.

4.Add the chicken to the wok, and stir-fry for 3 to 4 minutes or until lightly browned.

5.Stir the sauce, add to the skillet, and stir fry for 1 to 2 minutes until the sauce thickens. Serve immediately, topped with the toasted coconut and macadamia nuts.

 NUTRITIONAL VALUE

Kcal	Carbs	Protein	Total Fat	Sat. Fat	Cholesterol
301	18g	31g	12g	4g	73mg

CHICKEN THIGH CACCIATORE

SERVINGS	PREPARATION TIME	COOKING TIME
2	10 Mins	40-45 Mins

Ingredients

- ·2 tsp (10ml) olive oil
- ·2 (3-oz) (85g) boneless, skinless chicken thighs
- ·½ cup (40g) chopped sweet onion
- ·2 beetrootss stalks, diced
- ·2 courgettes, sliced
- ·1 red bell pepper, sliced
- ·1 carrot, diced
- ·1 tsp (3g) minced garlic
- ·2 cups (180g) low-sodium diced tomatoes
- ·½ cup (120ml) low-sodium chicken broth
- ·2 tbsp (30ml) low-sodium tomato paste
- ·2 tsp (4g) chopped fresh basil
- ·Pinch of red pepper flakes
- ·4-oz (110g) dry no-yolk egg noodles

Directions

1.In your medium skillet, heat the olive oil over medium-high heat. Add the chicken and cook for 12 to 15 minutes until just cooked through, turning several times.

2.Add the onions, beetrootss, courgette, bell pepper, carrots, and garlic, then sauté for 5 minutes.

3.Stir in the tomatoes, broth, tomato paste, basil, and red pepper flakes. Bring the sauce to a boil, then adjust to low heat and simmer within 20 minutes, covered, until the chicken is tender.

4.Prepare the noodles according to the package instructions. Serve cacciatore over the egg noodles.

 NUTRITIONAL VALUE

Kcal	Carbs	Protein	Total Fat	Sat. Fat	Cholesterol
458	60g	30g	9g	1g	81mg

MUSTARD-ROASTED ALMOND CHICKEN TENDERS

SERVINGS
2

PREPARATION TIME
15 Mins

COOKING TIME
15 Mins

Ingredients

- ·1/8 cup (30ml) low-sodium yellow mustard
- ·1 tsp (3g) yellow mustard seed
- ·1/8 (0,5g) tsp dry mustard
- ·1/8 tsp (0,5g) garlic powder
- ·1 egg white
- ·1 tbsp (15ml) fresh lemon juice
- ·1/8 cup (20g) almond flour
- ·1/8 cup (20g) ground almonds
- ·1/2-pound (220g) chicken tenders

Directions

1.Preheat the oven to 400°F (200°C). Place a wire rack on your baking sheet.

2.In a shallow bowl, combine the yellow mustard, mustard seed, ground mustard, garlic powder, egg white, and lemon juice.

3.To a plate or shallow bowl, add the almond flour and ground almonds, and combine.

4.Dip the chicken tenders into the mustard-egg mixture, then into the almond mixture to coat. Place each tender on the rack on the baking pan as you work.

5.Bake the chicken within 12 to 15 minutes until golden brown. Serve immediately.

 NUTRITIONAL VALUE

Kcal	Carbs	Protein	Total Fat	Sat. Fat	Cholesterol
166	2g	29g	4g	0g	66mg

BALSAMIC ROSEMARY CHICKEN

SERVINGS
2

PREPARATION TIME
10 Mins + chilling time

COOKING TIME
40 Mins

Ingredients

- ·½ cup (120ml) balsamic vinegar, + 2 tbsp (30ml)
- ·1 tsp (5ml) olive oil
- ·1 tbsp (6g) chopped fresh rosemary
- ·1 garlic clove, minced
- ·⅛ tsp (0,5g) salt
- ·Freshly ground black pepper to taste
- ·Olive oil cooking spray
- ·2 (6-oz) (170g) boneless, skinless chicken breasts
- ·Fresh rosemary sprigs for garnish

Directions

1. Combine 1/2 cup balsamic vinegar, olive oil, rosemary, garlic, salt, and pepper in a small pot.
2. Bring to a boil, then reduce to a medium heat for 3 minutes, or until reduced by half. Refrigerate the pan for 15 minutes or place it in the freezer for 5 minutes.
3. Spray a 9-by-9-inch (23 x 23 cm) baking dish with nonstick cooking spray. Place the chicken in the baking dish and pour over the cooled marinade. Set aside for 30 minutes.
4. Preheat the oven to 400 degrees Fahrenheit. Remove the dish from the refrigerator, cover with aluminum foil, and bake the chicken for 35 minutes in the marinade.
5. Transfer the chicken to plates to serve. Fill a small pot halfway with the prepared marinade.
6. Add the remaining balsamic vinegar and continue to boil for 3 to 5 minutes, or until the sauce thickens. Serve the sauce over the chicken, topped with fresh rosemary.

 NUTRITIONAL VALUE

Kcal	Carbs	Protein	Total Fat	Sat. Fat	Cholesterol
228	2g	49g	4g	2g	97mg

TANDOORI TURKEY PIZZAS

SERVINGS	PREPARATION TIME	COOKING TIME
2	15 Mins	18 Mins

Ingredients

- ·2 (6½-inch) (16cm) whole-wheat pita bread
- ·½ tsp (3ml) olive oil
- ·1 small onion, chopped
- ·2 cloves garlic, minced
- ·1/4-pound (110g) ground turkey
- ·4 oz (110g) canned no-salt-added tomato sauce
- ·1 tsp (5g) curry powder
- ·¼ tsp (1g) smoked paprika
- ·1/8 tsp (0,5g) ground cumin
- ·1/8 tsp (0,5g) cayenne pepper
- ·1/8 cup (30g) crumbled feta cheese
- ·1 ½ tbsp (15g) low-fat plain Greek yogurt

Directions

1.Preheat the oven to 425°F (220°C). Place the pita bread on your baking sheet lined with aluminum foil and set aside.

2.In your large skillet, heat the olive oil over medium heat. Add the onion and garlic, then cook for 2 minutes, stirring frequently.

3.Add the ground turkey and sauté, breaking up the meat. Cook for 5 minutes or until the turkey is no longer pink.

4.Add the tomato sauce, curry powder, paprika, cumin, and cayenne pepper to the sauce and bring to a simmer. Simmer over low heat for 1 minute.

5.Top the pita "pizzas" evenly with the turkey mixture. Sprinkle each with the feta cheese.

6.Bake within 10 to 12 minutes or until the pizzas are hot. Drizzle each pizza with the yogurt and serve immediately.

 NUTRITIONAL VALUE

Kcal	Carbs	Protein	Total Fat	Sat. Fat	Cholesterol
308	43g	24g	6g	2g	40mg

TURKEY AND MANGO LETTUCE WRAPS

SERVINGS
2

PREPARATION TIME
20 Mins

COOKING TIME
0 Mins

Ingredients

- ·1 cup (90g) chopped cooked turkey
- ·1 cup (90g) low-sodium canned black beans, rinsed and drained
- ·½ avocado, diced
- ·1 scallion, white and green parts, chopped
- ·1 tsp (5ml) freshly squeezed lime juice
- ·1 tsp (3g) chopped fresh coriander
- ·¼ tsp (1g) ground cumin
- ·4 large Boston lettuce leaves
- ·½ mango, diced, for garnish

Directions

1.In a medium bowl, mix the turkey, black beans, avocado, green onions, lime juice, coriander, and cumin until well combined.
2.Spoon the filling evenly between the lettuce leaves and top with mango. Serve.

 NUTRITIONAL VALUE

Kcal	Carbs	Protein	Total Fat	Sat. Fat	Cholesterol
368	40g	30g	11g	2g	53mg

GRILLED TURKEY AND VEGGIE KABOBS

SERVINGS	PREPARATION TIME	COOKING TIME
2	20 Mins	10 Mins

Ingredients

- ·1/2-pound (220g) turkey tenderloin, cut into 1-inch cubes
- ·Pinch of salt
- ·⅛ tsp (0,5g) cayenne pepper
- ·1/2 yellow summer squash, cut into ½-inch (1,5cm) slices
- ·1/2 orange bell pepper, seeded & cut into 1-inch cubes
- ·1/2 red bell pepper, seeded and cut into 1-inch cubes
- ·1 1/2 green onions, cut into 2- inch pieces
- ·1/8 cup (30g) apple jelly
- ·1 tbsp (15ml) fresh lemon juice
- ·½ tbsp (5g) butter
- ·½ tbsp (5g) low-sodium mustard
- ·½ tsp (2g) dried oregano leaves

Directions

1. Heat the grill to medium-high.
2. On a platter, season the turkey with salt and cayenne pepper.
3. Thread the turkey cubes onto kabob skewers, alternating with the squash, orange bell pepper, red bell pepper, and scallion.
4. In a small saucepan, combine apple jelly, lemon juice, and butter. Cook for 2 minutes over low heat, or until the apple jelly melts and the mixture is smooth. Combine the mustard and oregano in a mixing bowl.
5. Brush the kabobs with the apple jelly mixture and place them on the hot grill for 4 minutes.
6. Uncover, turn the kabobs, and brush with extra apple jelly mixture. Return to the grill for 3 minutes.
7. Uncover the grill and cook the kabobs for 2 to 3 minutes more, brushing with the leftover apple jelly mixture.

 NUTRITIONAL VALUE

Kcal	Carbs	Protein	Total Fat	Sat. Fat	Cholesterol
232	21g	30g	5g	2g	53mg

LEMON TARRAGON TURKEY MEDALLIONS

SERVINGS	PREPARATION TIME	COOKING TIME
2	15 Mins	10 Mins

Ingredients

- ·1/2-pound (220g) turkey tenderloin
- ·Pinch of salt
- ·1/8 tsp (0,5g) lemon pepper
- ·1 tbsp (8g) cornstarch
- ·½ tsp (2g) dried tarragon leaves
- ·1/8 cup (30ml) fresh lemon juice
- ·1/4 cup (60ml) low-sodium chicken stock
- ·½ tsp (2g) grated fresh lemon zest
- ·1 tsp (5ml) olive oil

Directions

1.Cut the turkey tenderloin crosswise into ½-inch (1,5cm) slices. Sprinkle with salt and lemon pepper.

2.In a small bowl, combine the cornstarch, tarragon, lemon juice, chicken stock, and lemon zest.

3.Heat the olive oil in your large nonstick skillet over medium heat. Add the turkey tenderloins. Cook within 2 minutes, then turn and cook for another 2 minutes.

4.Add the lemon juice mixture to the skillet. Cook, frequently stirring until the sauce boils and thickens and the turkey is cooked. Serve immediately.

 NUTRITIONAL VALUE

Kcal	Carbs	Protein	Total Fat	Sat. Fat	Cholesterol
169	5g	29g	3g	1g	70mg

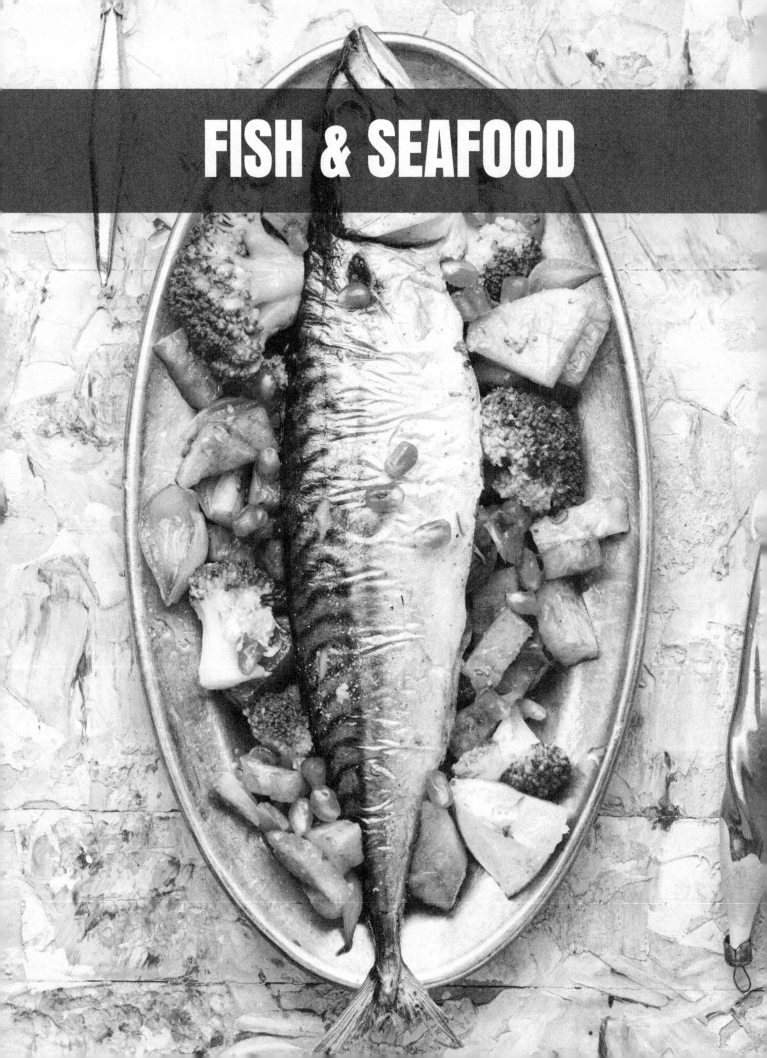

FISH & SEAFOOD

COD SCAMPI

SERVINGS
2

PREPARATION TIME
10 Mins

COOKING TIME
15-20 Mins

Ingredients

- ·1 tsp (5ml) olive oil
- ·2 cloves garlic, minced
- ·1/8 cup (30ml) fresh lemon juice
- ·1/8 cup (30ml) white wine or fish stock
- ·½ tsp(2g) fresh lemon zest
- ·Pinch of salt
- ·1/8 tsp (1g) lemon pepper
- ·2 (6-oz) (170g) cod fillets
- ·1 scallion, minced
- ·1 ½ tbsp (3g) minced flat-leaf fresh parsley

Directions

1.Preheat the oven to 400°F (200°C). Line a baking pan with parchment paper.

2.In your small bowl, combine the olive oil, garlic, lemon juice, white wine, lemon zest, salt, and lemon pepper.

3.Arrange the fillets' skin side down on the prepared baking pan. Pour the lemon juice mixture over your fillets.

4.Roast within 15 to 20 minutes or until the fish flakes. Serve the fish with the pan drippings, sprinkled with the scallions and parsley.

 NUTRITIONAL VALUE

Kcal	Carbs	Protein	Total Fat	Sat. Fat	Cholesterol
212	3g	35g	5g	1g	62mg

VIETNAMESE FISH AND NOODLE BOWL

SERVINGS
2

PREPARATION TIME
15 Mins

COOKING TIME
15 Mins

Ingredients

- ·1/2-pound (220g) **sea bass** fillets, cut into 1-inch (2,5cm) pieces
- ·1 tbsp (8g) cornstarch
- ·⅛ tsp (0,5) cayenne pepper
- ·2 tsp (10ml) fish sauce
- ·1 tbsp (15ml) rice wine vinegar
- ·1 tsp (6g) sugar
- ·2 tbsp (30ml) fresh lemon juice
- ·1 tsp (5ml) olive oil
- ·¼ cup (20) minced daikon radish
- ·3 cloves garlic, minced
- ·4 oz (110g) whole-wheat spaghetti, broken in half
- ·1½ cups (350ml) low-sodium vegetable broth
- ·2 tbsp (15g) chopped peanuts
- ·2 tbsp (5g) minced fresh coriander
- ·2 tbsp (5g) minced fresh basil

Directions

1.In a medium bowl, toss the **sea bass** with the cornstarch and cayenne pepper and set aside.

2.In a small bowl, combine the fish sauce, rice wine vinegar, sugar, and lemon juice.

3.In your large skillet, heat the olive oil over medium heat. Add the daikon and garlic and cook for 1 minute, stirring constantly.

4.Add the fish to the skillet; sauté for 2 to 3 minutes, frequently stirring, until the fish browns lightly. Remove the fish mixture to a large bowl and set aside.

5.Add the spaghetti and vegetable broth to the skillet, and stir. Let it simmer over high heat and cook within 7 to 8 minutes or until the pasta is al dente.

6.Return the fish and radish mixture to the skillet along with the fish sauce mixture, peanuts, coriander, and basil. Toss for 1 minute, then serve immediately in bowls.

 NUTRITIONAL VALUE

Kcal	Carbs	Protein	Total Fat	Sat. Fat	Cholesterol
324	38g	30g	6g	1g	46mg

ROASTED HADDOCK WITH BROCCOLI

SERVINGS
2

PREPARATION TIME
10 Mins

COOKING TIME
22 Mins

Ingredients

- ·1 cup (90g) broccoli florets
- ·2 tbsp (30ml) olive oil, divided
- ·2 (6-oz) (170g) haddock fillets
- ·1/2 cup (60g) cherry tomatoes
- ·1 clove of peeled garlic, sliced
- ·1/8 tsp (0,5g) white pepper
- ·½ tsp (3g) paprika
- ·1 tbsp (15ml) fresh lemon juice
- ·1 tbsp (10g) crumbled feta cheese

Directions

1. Preheat the oven to 400°F (200°C). Line a baking sheet with parchment paper.
2. Place the broccoli florets on the prepared baking sheet. Drizzle with 1 tbsp olive oil and toss to coat. Spread the broccoli in one layer, and roast the broccoli for 10 minutes.
3. Remove the baking sheet from the oven. Move the broccoli over to make room for the fish.
4. Place the fish, cherry tomatoes, and garlic on the baking sheet. Sprinkle the fish with the white pepper and paprika.
5. In your small bowl, combine the lemon juice and the remaining olive oil, and drizzle over the fish and vegetable mixture.
6. Roast for 10 to 12 minutes longer until the fish flakes. Sprinkle with the feta cheese and serve immediately.

 NUTRITIONAL VALUE

Kcal	Carbs	Protein	Total Fat	Sat. Fat	Cholesterol
258	6g	33g	11g	2g	72mg

HADDOCK TACOS WITH SPICY SLAW

SERVINGS	PREPARATION TIME	COOKING TIME
2	15 Mins	12 Mins

Ingredients

- ·1 cup (30g) shredded cabbage
- ·1 carrot, shredded
- ·½ scallion, white and green parts, finely chopped
- ·¼ cup (60ml) fat-free sour cream
- ·2 tsp (10ml) sriracha sauce
- ·1 tsp (5ml) freshly squeezed lime juice
- ·2 (5-oz) (140g) haddock fillets
- ·¼ tsp (1g) ground cumin
- ·Sea salt & ground black pepper to taste
- ·Nonstick olive oil cooking spray
- ·4 (6-inch) (15cm) corn tortillas at room temperature

Directions

1. Toss the cabbage, carrots, green onions, sour cream, sriracha, and lime juice in a medium mixing bowl until well combined. Place aside.
2. Season the haddock with cumin, salt, and pepper all over.
3. Spray a medium skillet thoroughly with cooking spray and heat it over medium-high heat. Cook for 6 minutes per side, rotating once, until the haddock is totally done.
4. Fill the tortillas with the fish and top with the spicy slaw. Serve.

 NUTRITIONAL VALUE

Kcal	Carbs	Protein	Total Fat	Sat. Fat	Cholesterol
305	37g	31g	3g	0g	72mg

SALMON WITH FARRO PILAF

SERVINGS

2

PREPARATION TIME

10 Mins

COOKING TIME

25 Mins

Ingredients

- ·1/4 cup (25g) farro
- ·3/4 cup (180ml) low-sodium vegetable broth
- ·2 (4-oz) (110g) salmon fillets
- ·Pinch of salt
- ·¼ tsp (1g) dried marjoram leaves
- ·⅛ tsp (0,5g) white pepper
- ·1/8 cup (15g) dried cherries
- ·1/8 cup (15g) dried currants
- ·1/2 cup (10g) fresh baby spinach leaves
- ·1/2 tbsp (8ml) orange juice

Directions

1.Preheat the oven to 400°F (200°C). Line your baking sheet using parchment paper and set aside.

2.In your medium saucepan over medium heat, combine the farro and the vegetable broth and bring to a simmer. Adjust to low heat and simmer for 25 minutes, partially covered, or until the farro is tender.

3.Meanwhile, sprinkle the salmon with the salt, marjoram, and white pepper and place it on the prepared baking sheet.

4.When the farro has cooked for 10 minutes, bake the salmon in the oven for 12 to 15 minutes until the salmon flakes. Remove and cover to keep warm.

5.When the farro is tender, add the cherries, currants, spinach, and orange juice; stir and cover. Let stand off the heat for 2 to 3 minutes. Plate the salmon and serve with the farro pilaf.

 NUTRITIONAL VALUE

Kcal	Carbs	Protein	Total Fat	Sat. Fat	Cholesterol
304	32g	26g	8g	1g	62mg

SESAME-CRUSTED TUNA STEAKS

SERVINGS	PREPARATION TIME	COOKING TIME
2	5 Mins	6 Mins

Ingredients

- ·Olive oil nonstick cooking spray
- ·½ tbsp (8ml) olive oil
- ·1 tsp (5ml) sesame oil
- ·2 (6-oz) (170g) ahi tuna steaks
- ·6 tbsp (50g) sesame seeds
- ·Salt & ground black pepper to taste

Directions

1.Preheat the oven to 450°F (230°C) and lightly spray a baking sheet with cooking spray.

2.In your small bowl, stir together the olive oil and sesame oil. Brush the tuna steaks with the oil mixture.

3.Put the sesame seeds in a shallow bowl. Press the steaks into the seeds, turning to cover all sides.

4.Place the tuna steaks on the prepared baking sheet. Sprinkle with salt and pepper.

5.Bake for 4 to 6 minutes per ½-inch (1,5cm) thickness or until the fish flakes when tested with a fork. Serve immediately.

 NUTRITIONAL VALUE

Kcal	Carbs	Protein	Total Fat	Sat. Fat	Cholesterol
520	6g	56g	30g	1g	83mg

LEMON GARLIC MACKEREL

SERVINGS
2

PREPARATION TIME
10 Mins

COOKING TIME
5 Mins

Ingredients

- ·2 (4-oz) (110g) mackerel fillets
- ·Salt to taste
- ·2 garlic cloves, minced
- ·Juice of ½ lemon
- ·Freshly ground black pepper to taste

Directions

1.Line your baking sheet using aluminum foil and lay the fillets on it. Sprinkle them with salt and leave them for 5 minutes.

2.Mix the garlic, lemon juice, and some pepper in your small bowl. Pour the mixture over the mackerel.

3.Meanwhile, preheat the broiler—broil within 5 minutes or until the fish is opaque. Serve immediately.

 NUTRITIONAL VALUE

Kcal	Carbs	Protein	Total Fat	Sat. Fat	Cholesterol
302	1g	27g	20g	2g	85mg

STEAMED COD ROLLS WITH GREENS

SERVINGS	PREPARATION TIME	COOKING TIME
2	15 Mins	11 Mins

Ingredients

- ·2 (6-oz) (170g) cod fillets
- ·2 tsp (5g) grated peeled fresh ginger root
- ·2 cloves garlic, minced
- ·1 tsp (5ml) low-sodium soy sauce
- ·½ tbsp (8ml) rice wine vinegar
- ·½ tsp (3ml) toasted sesame oil
- ·1 cup (20g) fresh torn spinach leaves
- ·1/2 cup (10g) fresh stemmed torn kale
- ·1/2 cup (20g) sliced mushrooms
- ·1 tsp (4g) toasted sesame seeds

Directions

1.Cut the cod fillets in half lengthwise. Sprinkle each piece with some ginger root and garlic. Roll up the fillets and ginger root side in. Fasten with a toothpick and set aside.

2.In your small bowl, combine the soy sauce, vinegar, and toasted sesame oil.

3.Boil water over medium heat in a large shallow saucepan that will hold your steamer.

4.Arrange the spinach leaves and kale in the bottom of the steamer. Add the rolled cod fillets. Add the mushrooms, and sprinkle with the soy sauce mixture.

5.Cover and steam for 7 to 11 minutes until the fish is cooked. Remove the toothpicks.

6.Sprinkle with the sesame seeds and serve the fish on top of the wilted greens and mushrooms.

 NUTRITIONAL VALUE

Kcal	Carbs	Protein	Total Fat	Sat. Fat	Cholesterol
263	7g	36g	8g	2g	81mg

GRILLED SCALLOPS WITH GREMOLATA

SERVINGS

2

PREPARATION TIME

15 Mins

COOKING TIME

6 Mins

Ingredients

- ·10 sea scallops
- ·1 scallion, cut into pieces
- ·1/2 cup (20g) packed fresh flat-leaf parsley
- ·1/8 cup (4g) packed fresh basil leaves
- ·½ tsp (3g) lemon zest
- ·1 ½ tbsp (25ml) fresh lemon juice
- ·½ tbsp (8ml) olive oil
- ·1 tsp (4g) butter, melted
- ·Pinch of salt
- ·⅛ tsp (0,5g)lemon pepper

Directions

1.Prepare and preheat the grill to medium-high. Make sure the grill rack is clean.

2.Meanwhile, in a blender, blend the green onions, parsley, basil, lemon zest, lemon juice, and olive oil until the herbs are finely chopped. Pour into your small bowl and set aside.

3.Put the scallops on a plate, and brush it with the melted butter. Sprinkle with the salt and the lemon pepper.

4.Place a sheet of heavy-duty foil on the grill, punch some holes in it, and arrange the scallops evenly across it.

5.Grill the scallops for 2 to 3 minutes per side, turning once, until opaque. Drizzle with the gremolata and serve.

 NUTRITIONAL VALUE

Kcal	Carbs	Protein	Total Fat	Sat. Fat	Cholesterol
190	2g	28g	7g	2g	68mg

SHRIMP AND PINEAPPLE LETTUCE WRAPS

SERVINGS

2

PREPARATION TIME

15 Mins

COOKING TIME

12 Mins

Ingredients

- ·1 tsp (5ml) olive oil
- ·1 jalapeño pepper, seeded & minced
- ·3 green onions, chopped
- ·1 yellow bell pepper, seeded & chopped
- ·4 oz (110g) small shrimp, peeled & deveined
- ·1 cup (80g) canned pineapple chunks, drained, reserving juice
- ·1 tbsp (15ml) fresh lime juice
- ·Half of 1 avocado, peeled and cubed
- ·1 small carrot, coarsely grated
- ·4 romaine or Boston lettuce leaves, rinsed and dried

Directions

1.In your medium saucepan, heat the olive oil over medium heat. Add the jalapeño pepper and green onions and cook for 2 minutes, stirring constantly. 2.Add the bell pepper, and cook for 2 minutes. Add the shrimp, and cook within 1 minute, stirring constantly.

3.Add the pineapple, 2 tablespoons of the reserved pineapple juice, and lime juice, and bring to a simmer.

4.Simmer for 1-minute longer or until the shrimp curl and turn pink. Let the mixture cool for 5 minutes.

5.Serve the shrimp mixture with the cubed avocado and grated carrot, wrapped in the lettuce leaves.

 NUTRITIONAL VALUE

Kcal	Carbs	Protein	Total Fat	Sat. Fat	Cholesterol
241	29g	6g	9g	2g	109mg

SALADS & SIDES

GREEN RICE SALAD WITH TOMATOES

SERVINGS
2

PREPARATION TIME
15 Mins

COOKING TIME
10 Mins

Ingredients

- ·1 (10-oz) (280g) package of cooked brown rice
- ·1 tbsp (15ml) olive oil
- ·1 tbsp (15ml) fresh lemon juice
- ·½ tbsp (8ml) orange juice
- ·½ tbsp (8ml) pure maple syrup
- ·Pinch of salt
- ·1/4 cup (5g) chopped fresh flat-leaf parsley
- ·1/8 cup (4g) chopped fresh basil leaves
- ·½ tbsp (3g) fresh thyme leaves
- ·5 oz (140g) package of frozen baby peas, thawed
- ·1/2 cup (30g) sliced beetrootss ·1 cup (60g) grape tomatoes

Directions

1. Thaw the brown rice according to the package directions.
2. Meanwhile, in your large salad bowl, combine the olive oil, lemon juice, orange juice, maple syrup, salt, parsley, basil, and thyme, and mix well.
3. Add the cooked brown rice and toss to coat. Stir in the peas, beetrootss, and tomatoes and toss again. Serve.

 NUTRITIONAL VALUE

Kcal	Carbs	Protein	Total Fat	Sat. Fat	Cholesterol
305	50g	9g	9g	1g	0mg

LEMONY BULGUR, LENTIL, AND CUCUMBER SALAD

SERVINGS
2

PREPARATION TIME
15 Mins + chilling time

COOKING TIME
0 Mins

Ingredients

- ·2 cups (200g) cooked bulgur
- ·1 cup (100g) low-sodium canned lentils, rinsed and drained
- ·1 English cucumber, diced
- ·½ jalapeño pepper, chopped
- ·½ scallion, white and green parts, thinly sliced
- ·½ red bell pepper, finely chopped
- ·Juice and zest of 1 lemon
- ·1 tbsp (8g) granulated sugar
- ·1 tbsp (4g) chopped fresh coriander
- ·2 tbsp (15g) chopped roasted peanuts for garnish

Directions

1.In a large bowl, toss together the bulgur, lentils, cucumber, jalapeño, scallion, and bell pepper until well mixed.

2.Add the lemon juice, lemon zest, sugar, and coriander and toss to coat. Cover your bowl and let the salad chill for 30 minutes in the refrigerator. Serve topped with chopped peanuts.

 NUTRITIONAL VALUE

Kcal	Carbs	Protein	Total Fat	Sat. Fat	Cholesterol
392	75g	20g	5g	1g	0mg

MIXED BERRY CHICKEN SALAD

SERVINGS	PREPARATION TIME	COOKING TIME
2	15 Mins	8 Mins

Ingredients

- ·2 (6-oz) (170g) boneless, skinless chicken breasts, cubed
- ·Pinch of salt
- ·⅛ tsp (0,5g) white pepper
- ·2 tsp (10ml) olive oil, divided
- ·1 cup (125g) sliced strawberries
- ·1 cup (125g) blueberries
- ·1/2 cup (70g) blackberries
- ·1/8 cup (30g) low-fat plain Greek yogurt
- ·1 ½ tbsp (25ml) fresh lime juice
- ·1 tbsp (15ml) honey
- ·½ tsp (3g) grated fresh lime zest
- ·1/2 cup (60g) raspberries
- ·2 cups (40g) mixed green lettuce

Directions

1.Sprinkle the chicken breasts with salt plus pepper.

2.Heat 1 teaspoon of olive oil in a large nonstick skillet. Add the chicken and cook for 5 to 7 minutes, frequently stirring, until lightly browned. Transfer to a clean plate.

3.In your large bowl, combine the strawberries, blueberries, and blackberries and gently toss to mix.

4.In your small bowl, combine the yogurt, lime juice, honey, lime zest, and remaining olive oil.

5.Add the chicken to the berry mixture, and drizzle the yogurt mixture over all the ingredients. Toss gently.

6.Top the chicken salad with the raspberries. Serve on a bed of mixed green lettuce.

 NUTRITIONAL VALUE

Kcal	Carbs	Protein	Total Fat	Sat. Fat	Cholesterol
394	42g	43g	6g	1g	99mg

WARM SOBA AND TOFU SALAD

SERVINGS
2

PREPARATION TIME
20 Mins

COOKING TIME
10 Mins

Ingredients

- ·4 oz (110g) soba noodles
- ·1 ½ tbsp (25ml) orange juice
- ·1 tbsp (8g) low-sodium yellow mustard
- ·½ tbsp (8ml) fresh lemon juice
- ·½ tbsp (8ml) pure maple syrup
- ·½ tsp (3g) dried thyme leaves
- ·⅛ tsp (0,5g) black pepper
- ·½ tbsp (8ml) sesame oil
- ·4 oz (110g) firm tofu, drained and cut into 1-inch pieces
- ·1 1/2 (30g) cups chopped red cabbage
- ·Half of 1 red bell pepper, seeded and chopped
- ·1 small carrot, grated
- ·1 ½ scallion, chopped
- ·2 cups (40g) mixed salad greens

Directions

1.Boil a large pot of water. Add the soba noodles and cook as stated in the package directions. Drain, rinse with warm water, drain again, and put into a serving bowl.

2.Meanwhile, in a small bowl, combine the orange juice, mustard, lemon juice, maple syrup, thyme, and black pepper, and mix well.

3.Heat your large nonstick skillet over medium heat. Add the sesame oil and tofu cubes, then cook for 2 minutes, stirring occasionally.

4.Add the cabbage, red bell pepper, and carrot; cook and stir within 3 to 4 minutes longer. Add the orange juice mixture and bring to a simmer.

5.Place the tofu, vegetable mixture, and green onions in the serving bowl with the soba noodles and toss. Serve over the salad greens.

 NUTRITIONAL VALUE

Kcal	Carbs	Protein	Total Fat	Sat. Fat	Cholesterol
335	60g	16g	7g	1g	0mg

FRUITED QUINOA SALAD

SERVINGS	PREPARATION TIME	COOKING TIME
2	10 Mins	20 Mins

Ingredients

- ·1/2 cup (60g) quinoa
- ·1 cup (240ml) water
- ·1 ½ tbsp (25ml) fresh lemon juice
- ·½ tbsp (8ml) pure honey
- ·1 tbsp (15ml) buttermilk
- ·1 tbsp (4g) chopped fresh mint
- ·1 cup (80g) red grape
- ·1/2 cup (60g) cherries, pitted
- ·1 cup (120) fresh blueberries
- ·1/8 cup (30g) crumbled goat cheese

Directions

1.Put the quinoa in your strainer and rinse well under cool running water.
2.In your medium saucepan, combine the quinoa and the water and let it boil over high heat.
3.Adjust to low heat and simmer for 15 to 18 minutes or until the liquid is absorbed. Put the quinoa in a salad bowl.
4.Meanwhile, in a small bowl, combine the lemon juice, honey, buttermilk, and mint, and mix well. Pour the quinoa into the bowl and toss.
5.Add the grapes, cherries, and blueberries and toss to coat. Top with the goat cheese and serve.

 NUTRITIONAL VALUE

Kcal	Carbs	Protein	Total Fat	Sat. Fat	Cholesterol
272	55g	9g	4g	1g	5mg

TUNISIAN SPICED CARROTS

SERVINGS
2

PREPARATION TIME
10 Mins

COOKING TIME
10 Mins

Ingredients

- ·1 tsp (5ml) olive oil
- ·½ tsp (3g) minced garlic
- ·½ tsp (3g) peeled, grated fresh ginger
- ·¼ tsp (1g) ground cumin
- ·⅛ tsp (0,5g) ground coriander
- ·3 large carrots, thinly sliced
- ·¼ cup (60ml) low-sodium vegetable broth
- ·Juice of ½ lemon
- ·1 tbsp (15ml) honey
- ·Sea salt to taste

Directions

1.In a medium saucepan, warm the olive oil over medium-high heat. Add the garlic, ginger, cumin, and coriander, then sauté for 2 minutes until fragrant and softened.

2.Stir in the carrots, broth, lemon juice, and honey. Boil the mixture, adjust to low heat and simmer for 6 to 8 minutes until the carrots are tender. Season with salt and serve.

 NUTRITIONAL VALUE

Kcal	Carbs	Protein	Total Fat	Sat. Fat	Cholesterol
103	20g	1g	3g	0g	0mg

ASPARAGUS WITH ALMOND

SERVINGS	PREPARATION TIME	COOKING TIME
2	10 Mins	5 Mins

Ingredients

- ·½ tsp (3ml) avocado oil
- ·½ cup (50g) finely chopped almonds
- ·Juice and zest of ½ lime
- ·Sea salt & ground black pepper to taste
- ·½ pound (220g) asparagus, woody ends trimmed

Directions

1.In a small skillet, warm the olive oil over medium heat. Add the almonds and sauté for 4 minutes until they are fragrant and golden brown.

2.Remove and stir in the lime zest and juice. Season the almond mixture with salt and pepper and set aside.

3.Fill your medium saucepan with water and boil over high heat. Blanch the asparagus for 2 minutes until tender-crisp.

4.Drain the asparagus and arrange it on a serving plate. Sprinkle the almond topping over the vegetables and serve.

 NUTRITIONAL VALUE

Kcal	Carbs	Protein	Total Fat	Sat. Fat	Cholesterol
192	11g	8g	15g	1g	0mg

SKILLET-ROASTED SWEET POTATOES

SERVINGS
2

PREPARATION TIME
10 Mins

COOKING TIME
20 Mins

Ingredients

- ·1 medium sweet potato, cut into bite-sized pieces
- ·½ tbsp (8ml) fresh lemon juice
- ·1 tsp (5ml) olive oil
- ·Pinch of salt
- ·⅛ tsp (0,5g) white pepper
- ·1 1/2 chopped fresh flat-leaf parsley

Directions

1.Sprinkle the potatoes with lemon juice.

2.Heat the olive oil in your large nonstick skillet over medium heat. Add the potatoes, and sprinkle with the salt and white pepper.

3.Cook the potatoes within 15 to 20 minutes, stirring often, or until they are tender when pierced with a fork and the outsides are crisp.

4.Remove from the heat, sprinkle with the parsley, and serve immediately.

 NUTRITIONAL VALUE

Kcal	Carbs	Protein	Total Fat	Sat. Fat	Cholesterol
78	14g	1g	2g	0g	0mg

PIQUANT HARICOT BEANS

SERVINGS	PREPARATION TIME	COOKING TIME
2	10 Mins	15 Mins

Ingredients

- ·1 tsp (5ml) olive oil
- ·½ cup (40g) chopped sweet onion
- ·½ jalapeño pepper, chopped
- ·1 tsp (3g) minced garlic
- ·1 (15-oz) (420g) can of low-sodium haricot beans, rinsed and drained
- ·¼ tsp (1g) ground cumin
- ·⅛ tsp (0,5g) ground coriander
- ·Sea salt & ground black pepper to taste
- ·1 tsp (3g) chopped fresh cilantro, for garnish

Directions

1.In a medium saucepan, warm the olive oil over medium-high heat. Add the onions, jalapeños, and garlic, then sauté for 4 minutes until softened.
2.Stir in the beans, cumin, and coriander, then sauté for 10 minutes until the beans are heated through. Season with salt and pepper and serve topped with cilantro.

 NUTRITIONAL VALUE

Kcal	Carbs	Protein	Total Fat	Sat. Fat	Cholesterol
291	51g	16g	4g	1g	0mg

LIME BRUSSELS SPROUTS

SERVINGS	PREPARATION TIME	COOKING TIME
2	10 Mins	10 Mins

Ingredients

- ·2 tsp (10ml) olive oil
- ·1/2-pound (110g) Brussels sprouts, quartered
- ·¼ tsp (1g) minced garlic
- ·Juice and zest of 1 lime
- ·Sea salt & ground black pepper to taste

Directions

1.In a medium skillet, warm the olive oil over medium-high heat. Add the Brussels sprouts and garlic, then sauté for 5 to 6 minutes until tender.
2.Stir in the lime juice and zest and sauté for 1 more minute. Season with salt and pepper and serve.

 NUTRITIONAL VALUE

Kcal	Carbs	Protein	Total Fat	Sat. Fat	Cholesterol
144	23g	8g	6g	1g	0mg

SNACKS

ROASTED LENTIL SNACK MIX

SERVINGS
2

PREPARATION TIME
5 Mins + soaking time

COOKING TIME
0 Mins

Ingredients

- ·1/2 cup (60g) dried red lentils
- ·1/2 cup (60g) whole unsalted shelled pistachios
- ·1/4 cup (20g) unsalted shelled sunflower seeds
- ·½ cup (40g) dried cherries
- ·½ cup (40g) dark chocolate chips

Directions

1.In your bowl, cover the lentils with water, and soak them for 1 hour. Drain.
2.Preheat the oven to 350°F (180°C).
3.Transfer the lentils to a clean kitchen towel and dab gently. Set aside for about 10 minutes to dry. Spread the lentils out on a large baking sheet.
4.Transfer your baking sheet to the oven, and bake, stirring once or twice, for 20 to 25 minutes or until the lentils are crisp.
5.Remove from the oven. Let it cool to room temperature. Transfer to a large bowl.
6.Add the pistachios, sunflower seeds, cherries, and chocolate chips. Toss to combine. Let it cool, and serve.

 NUTRITIONAL VALUE

Kcal	Carbs	Protein	Total Fat	Sat. Fat	Cholesterol
629	67g	23g	32g	7g	5mg

MIXED VEGETABLE CHIPS

SERVINGS	PREPARATION TIME	COOKING TIME
2	20 Mins	50 Mins

Ingredients

- ·Olive oil cooking spray
- ·1 medium beetroots, peeled & sliced
- ·1 small courgette, sliced ·1 small sweet potato, sliced
- ·Half of 1 small swede, peeled & sliced
- ·¼ tsp (1g) salt, + more to sweat the vegetables
- ·1/8 tsp (0,5g) dried rosemary

Directions

1.Preheat the oven to 300°F (150°C). Spray a baking sheet with cooking spray. Line a plate with paper towels.

2.Lay the beetrootss, courgette, sweet potato, and swede in one layer on a paper towel. Lightly salt, and let sit for 10 minutes.

3.Cover the vegetables with another paper towel, and blot away any moisture on top. Arrange the vegetables on the prepared baking sheet, and spray them with cooking spray.

4.Transfer your baking sheet to the oven, and cook within 30 to 40 minutes or until the vegetables have browned.

5.Flip the vegetables, and cook for 10 minutes or until crisp. Remove from the oven. Transfer to your prepared plate to drain any excess oil.

6.In your small bowl, mix the salt and rosemary. Lightly season the chips with rosemary salt before serving.

 NUTRITIONAL VALUE

Kcal	Carbs	Protein	Total Fat	Sat. Fat	Cholesterol
72	16g	2g	0g	0g	0mg

ASPARAGUS FRIES

SERVINGS
2

PREPARATION TIME
15 Mins

COOKING TIME
15 Mins

Ingredients

- ·½ bunch asparagus ends trimmed and spears cut in half
- ·1 tbsp (8g) ground flaxseed mixed with 3 tablespoons (45ml) water, or 1 beaten egg
- ·¼ cup (20g) bread crumbs
- ·1 tsp (4g) mustard powder
- ·½ tsp (2g) garlic powder
- ·⅛ tsp (0.5g) salt

Directions

1.Preheat the oven to 400°F (200°C) and line your baking sheet with parchment or a silicone baking mat.
2.Mix the ground flaxseed with the water (or egg) and allow it to sit for 5 minutes.
3.Combine the bread crumbs, mustard powder, garlic powder, and salt in your shallow bowl.
4.Dip each asparagus length into the flaxseed and water and then into the bread crumb mixture, then place them on your prepared baking sheet, being careful not to overcrowd them.
5.Bake for 15 minutes or until crispy and browned. Serve immediately.

 NUTRITIONAL VALUE

Kcal	Carbs	Protein	Total Fat	Sat. Fat	Cholesterol
119	16g	8g	4g	2g	82mg

SESAME-GARLIC EDAMAME

SERVINGS
2

PREPARATION TIME
10 Mins

COOKING TIME
3-5 Mins

Ingredients

- ·7 oz (200g) package of frozen edamame in their shells
- ·½ tbsp (8ml) canola or sunflower oil
- ·½ tbsp (8ml) toasted sesame oil
- ·2 garlic cloves, minced
- ·¼ tsp (1g) kosher salt
- ·1/8 tsp (0,5g) red pepper flakes (or more)

Directions

1.Boil your large pot of water over high heat. Add the edamame, and cook for 2 to 3 minutes to warm them up.

2.Meanwhile, heat the sunflower oil, sesame oil, garlic, salt, and red pepper flakes in your large skillet over medium heat for 1 to 2 minutes, then remove the pan.

3.Drain the edamame and add them to the skillet, tossing to combine. Serve.

 NUTRITIONAL VALUE

Kcal	Carbs	Protein	Total Fat	Sat. Fat	Cholesterol
173	8g	11g	12g	1g	0mg

SWEET POTATO FRIES

SERVINGS
2

PREPARATION TIME
10 Mins

COOKING TIME
25-30 Mins

Ingredients

- ·2 sweet potatoes, scrubbed
- ·1 tbsp (15ml) olive oil
- ·1 tsp (4g) garlic powder
- ·1 tsp (4g) paprika
- ·¼ tsp (1g) freshly ground black pepper
- ·⅛ tsp (0,5g) cayenne pepper
- ·⅛ tsp (0,5g) salt

Directions

1.Preheat the oven to 425°F (220°C).

2.Leaving the skins on and using a very sharp knife, cut the sweet potatoes into thin, even matchsticks.

3.Transfer the matchsticks to a large baking sheet and drizzle with the olive oil. Sprinkle with the garlic powder, paprika, black pepper, cayenne pepper, and salt and toss to coat.

4.Arrange the potatoes in a single layer to ensure they crisp up. Bake for 15 minutes and flip to cook the other side.

5.Bake within 10 to 15 minutes or until crispy and brown. Serve immediately.

 NUTRITIONAL VALUE

Kcal	Carbs	Protein	Total Fat	Sat. Fat	Cholesterol
334	65g	4g	8g	2g	0mg

GARLICKY KALE CHIPS

SERVINGS	PREPARATION TIME	COOKING TIME
2	10 Mins	15 Mins

Ingredients

- ·Half a bunch of curly kale, tear the leaves into squares
- ·1 tsp (5ml) extra-virgin olive oil
- ·1/8 tsp (0,5g) kosher salt
- ·1/8 tsp (0,5g) garlic powder (optional)

Directions

1.Preheat the oven to 325°F (165°C). Line your rimmed baking sheet using parchment paper.

2.Place the kale in your large bowl, and drizzle with the oil. Massage with your fingers for 1 to 2 minutes to coat well. Spread out on the baking sheet.

3.Cook for 8 minutes, then toss and cook for another 7 minutes until crispy. Sprinkle with salt and garlic powder (if using). Serve.

 NUTRITIONAL VALUE

Kcal	Carbs	Protein	Total Fat	Sat. Fat	Cholesterol
28	2g	1g	2g	0g	0mg

BAKED TORTILLA CHIPS

SERVINGS
2

PREPARATION TIME
5 Mins

COOKING TIME
13-15 Mins

Ingredients

- ·½ tbsp (8ml) canola or sunflower oil
- ·2 medium whole-wheat tortillas
- ·⅛ tsp (0,5g) coarse salt

Directions

1.Preheat the oven to 350°F (180°C).

2.Brush the oil onto both sides of each tortilla. Stack them on a large cutting board, and cut the entire stack at once, cutting the stack into 8 wedges of each tortilla.

3.Transfer the tortilla pieces to a rimmed baking sheet. Sprinkle a little salt over each chip. Bake for 10 minutes, and then flip the chips. Bake for another 3 to 5 minutes, until they're just starting to brown.

 NUTRITIONAL VALUE

Kcal	Carbs	Protein	Total Fat	Sat. Fat	Cholesterol
194	20g	4g	11g	2g	0mg

SPICY GUACAMOLE

SERVINGS
2

PREPARATION TIME
5 Mins

COOKING TIME
0 Mins

Ingredients

- ·Half of 1 ripe avocado, peeled, pitted, and mashed
- ·¾ tbsp (10ml) freshly squeezed lime juice
- ·½ tbsp (5g) minced jalapeño pepper, or to taste
- ·½ tbsp (5g) minced red onion
- ·½ tbsp (3g) chopped fresh coriander
- ·1 garlic clove, minced
- ·⅛ tsp (0,5g) kosher salt
- ·Freshly ground black pepper to taste

Directions

1.In a large bowl, combine the avocado, lime juice, jalapeño, onion, coriander, garlic, salt, and pepper. Serve.

 NUTRITIONAL VALUE

Kcal	Carbs	Protein	Total Fat	Sat. Fat	Cholesterol
61	4g	1g	5g	1g	0mg

CHEESY SPINACH DIP

SERVINGS

2

PREPARATION TIME

10 Mins

COOKING TIME

0 Mins

Ingredients

- ·1 cup (30g) thawed chopped frozen spinach
- ·½ cup (125g) fat-free cottage cheese
- ·2 tbsp (15g) chopped sweet onion
- ·¼ cup (25g) grated Parmesan cheese
- ·1 tsp (3g) minced garlic
- ·Sea salt & ground black pepper to taste

Directions

1.In your medium bowl, stir together the spinach, cottage cheese, onion, Parmesan cheese, and garlic until well combined. Season with salt and pepper.

2.Cover the dip in the refrigerator until you are ready to serve it. Serve with vegetables or pita bread.

 NUTRITIONAL VALUE

Kcal	Carbs	Protein	Total Fat	Sat. Fat	Cholesterol
79	7g	11g	2g	1g	7mg

SWEET POTATO AND HARICOT BEANS HUMMUS

SERVINGS

2

PREPARATION TIME

10 Mins

COOKING TIME

0 Mins

Ingredients

- ·1 cup (90g) mashed cooked sweet potato
- ·1 cup (90g) low-sodium canned haricot beans, rinsed & drained
- ·2 tbsp (15g) tahini
- ·2 tbsp (30ml) olive oil
- ·Juice of 1 lime
- ·½ tsp (3g) minced garlic
- ·¼ tsp (1g) ground cumin
- ·Sea salt to taste
- ·Chopped fresh cilantro for garnish
- ·Pita bread, baked tortilla crisps, or veggies for serving

Directions

1.In your food processor, add the sweet potato, beans, tahini, olive oil, lime juice, garlic, and cumin and purée until very smooth, scraping at least once.
2.Season with salt, top with cilantro, and serve with pita bread, baked tortilla crisps, or veggies.

 NUTRITIONAL VALUE

Kcal	Carbs	Protein	Total Fat	Sat. Fat	Cholesterol
396	41g	11g	23g	3g	0mg

DESSERTS

PUMPKIN PIE FRUIT LEATHERS

SERVINGS

2 (10 fruit leathers)

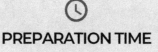

PREPARATION TIME

10 Mins

COOKING TIME

8 hours

Ingredients

- ·2 cups (150g) pumpkin purée
- ·1 cup (240ml) unsweetened applesauce
- ·1 tbsp (15ml) maple syrup
- ·¼ tsp (1g) ground cinnamon
- ·⅛ tsp (0,5g) ground nutmeg
- ·⅛ tsp (0,5g) ground ginger
- ·Pinch ground allspice

Directions

1.Preheat your oven to the lowest setting possible or 150F (75°C). Line your baking sheet with parchment paper and set aside.

2.In your medium bowl, whisk together the pumpkin, applesauce, maple syrup, cinnamon, nutmeg, ginger, and allspice until very well blended.

3.Spread the mixture on the baking sheet as evenly and thinly as possible.

4.Place your baking sheet in the oven and bake for 8 hours until the mixture is completely dried and no longer tacky to the touch. Remove the leather from the oven and cut it into 10 pieces.

 NUTRITIONAL VALUE

Kcal	Carbs	Protein	Total Fat	Sat. Fat	Cholesterol
33	8g	1g	0g	0g	0mg

SNOWY MERINGUES WITH BERRIES

SERVINGS
2

PREPARATION TIME
10 Mins + cooling time

COOKING TIME
45 Mins

Ingredients

- ·2 large egg whites at room temperature
- ·1 tsp (5ml) white vinegar
- ·½ tsp (3ml) pure vanilla extract
- ·⅛ tsp (0,5g) sea salt
- ·8 tbsp (140g) granulated sugar
- ·1 cup (120g) fresh mixed berries

Directions

1.Preheat the oven to 300°F (150°C). Line your baking sheet using parchment paper and set aside.

2.In your medium bowl, beat the egg whites, vinegar, vanilla, and salt with an electric mixer on medium speed for 5 minutes until soft peaks form.

3.Adjust to low speed and beat in the sugar, 1 tablespoon at a time, for 6 to 7 minutes until dissolved.

4.Drop 4 meringues onto the prepared sheet using a ½ cup measuring cup, leaving about 2 inches (5cm) between them. Use the back of your spoon to create a deep well in the middle of each meringue.

5.Place your baking sheet in the oven and bake for 45 minutes until the meringues are set, and then turn the oven off and let your meringues cool in the oven for two hours.

6.Remove the meringues from the oven and let them cool completely. Scoop the berries into the well in the center of the meringues and serve.

 NUTRITIONAL VALUE

Kcal	Carbs	Protein	Total Fat	Sat. Fat	Cholesterol
231	54g	4g	0g	0g	0mg

MANGO BLOOD ORANGE SORBET

SERVINGS	PREPARATION TIME	COOKING TIME
2	5 Mins	0 Mins

Ingredients

- ·1 cup (90g) frozen mango cubes
- ·1 tbsp (15ml) lemon juice
- ·1/8 cup (30ml) blood orange juice
- ·1 ½ tbsp (15g) sugar

Directions

1.In your high-speed blender or food processor, combine the mango, lemon juice, blood orange juice, and sugar, and process until smooth.
2.Serve immediately, or freeze for a denser texture.

 NUTRITIONAL VALUE

Kcal	Carbs	Protein	Total Fat	Sat. Fat	Cholesterol
100	26g	1g	0g	0g	0mg

PEACH MELBA FROZEN YOGURT PARFAITS

SERVINGS
2

PREPARATION TIME
15 Mins

COOKING TIME
5 Mins

Ingredients

- ·1 tbsp (10g) slivered almonds
- ·½ tbsp (6g) brown sugar
- ·1 peach, peeled & chopped
- ·1/2 cup (60g) fresh raspberries
- ·1 cup (250g) no-sugar-added vanilla frozen yogurt
- ·1 tbsp (15ml) peach jam
- ·1 tbsp (15ml) raspberry jam or preserves

Directions

1.Combine the almonds and brown sugar in your small nonstick skillet over medium heat.

2.Cook for 3 to 4 minutes, frequently stirring, until the sugar melts and coats the almonds. Remove from the heat and put the almonds on a plate to cool.

3.To make the parfaits: In four parfait or wine glasses, layer each with peaches, raspberries, frozen yogurt, peach jam, and raspberry jam. Top each glass with the caramelized almonds.

 NUTRITIONAL VALUE

Kcal	Carbs	Protein	Total Fat	Sat. Fat	Cholesterol
263	51g	7g	5g	1g	10mg

ALMOND CHEESECAKE-STUFFED APPLES

SERVINGS	**PREPARATION TIME**	**COOKING TIME**
2	15 Mins	25 Mins

Ingredients

- ·2 small apples, cut in half and cores scooped out on each side
- ·1 tsp (5ml) sunflower oil
- ·2 tbsp (25g) brown sugar, divided
- ·⅛ tsp (0,5g) ground cinnamon
- ·¼ cup (60g) fat-free cream cheese
- ·⅛ tsp (1ml) almond extract
- ·2 tbsp (15g) chopped almonds for garnish

Directions

1.Preheat the oven to 400°F (200°C). Line a small baking dish with parchment paper and arrange the apple halves in the dish, cut side up.

2.Brush the cut side of your apples with the sunflower oil. Sprinkle 1 tablespoon of brown sugar and the cinnamon over the halves. Place in your oven and bake for 15 minutes.

3.Meanwhile, stir together the cream cheese, remaining brown sugar, and almond extract in your small bowl until well blended.

4.Evenly divide the cream cheese mixture among the apple halves and bake for 10 more minutes. Top with almonds and serve.

 NUTRITIONAL VALUE

Kcal	Carbs	Protein	Total Fat	Sat. Fat	Cholesterol
307	42g	4g	16g	7g	22mg

TOFU MOCHA MOUSSE

SERVINGS
2

PREPARATION TIME
15 Mins (chilling time)

COOKING TIME
10 Mins

Ingredients

- ·4 oz (110g) 70-% dark chocolate, finely chopped
- ·¾ cup (180ml) unsweetened soy milk
- ·½ tsp (3g) espresso powder
- ·½ tsp (3ml) pure vanilla extract
- ·Pinch of sea salt
- ·4 oz (110g) silken tofu, drained well

Directions

1.Place the chocolate in your medium bowl and set aside.

2.In your small saucepan, warm the soy milk, espresso powder, vanilla, and salt over medium-high heat.

3.Boil the mixture and then pour it over the chocolate. Let the mixture stand for 10 minutes, then whisk until your chocolate is completely melted and the mixture is blended.

4.Pour the chocolate mixture into a food processor or blender and add the tofu. Pulse until very smooth.

5.Spoon the mousse into two bowls and refrigerate for 2 hours until firm. Serve.

 NUTRITIONAL VALUE

Kcal	Carbs	Protein	Total Fat	Sat. Fat	Cholesterol
441	23g	11g	38g	21g	0mg

PEANUT BUTTER AND CHIA PUDDING

SERVINGS	PREPARATION TIME	COOKING TIME
2	15 Mins (chilling time)	0 Mins

Ingredients

- ·2 cups (480ml) soy milk
- ·2 tbsp (25g) natural peanut butter
- ·2 tbsp (25g) brown sugar
- ·1 tsp (5ml) pure vanilla extract
- ·Pinch of sea salt
- ·½ cup (30g) chia seeds

Directions

1.In your medium bowl, whisk together the milk, peanut butter, brown sugar, vanilla, and salt until very smooth and well blended.

2.Stir in the chia seeds, cover the bowl, and refrigerate within 4 hours until the pudding is thick, stirring occasionally. Stir well and serve.

 NUTRITIONAL VALUE

Kcal	Carbs	Protein	Total Fat	Sat. Fat	Cholesterol
200	38g	17g	31g	3g	0mg

MAPLE-WALNUT POTS DE CRÈME

SERVINGS
2

PREPARATION TIME
10 Mins (chilling time)

COOKING TIME
5 Mins

Ingredients

- ·½ cup (120ml) unsweetened soy milk
- ·¼ tsp (1ml) pure vanilla extract
- ·1½ tsp (7g) unflavored gelatin
- ·½ cup (125g) fat-free vanilla Greek yogurt
- ·½ cup (125g) low-fat buttermilk
- ·⅓ cup (80ml) maple syrup
- ·Pinch of sea salt
- ·2 tbsp (15g) chopped walnuts, for garnish

Directions

1.In a small saucepan, stir the soy milk and vanilla over medium heat for 2 minutes until just warmer than room temperature.

2.Stir in the gelatin and heat the mixture for 3 minutes until scalded but not boiling. Remove the saucepan from the heat and set aside to cool for 10 minutes.

3.Whisk in the yogurt, buttermilk, maple syrup, and salt until well blended.

4.Pour the mixture into 2 (6-ounce) (170g) ramekins and chill for at least 4 hours, covered, in the refrigerator until completely set. Serve topped with walnuts.

 NUTRITIONAL VALUE

Kcal	Carbs	Protein	Total Fat	Sat. Fat	Cholesterol
301	49g	13g	6g	1g	5mg

LOADED SOY YOGURT BOWLS

SERVINGS

2

PREPARATION TIME

15 Mins

COOKING TIME

0 Mins

Ingredients

- ·2 cups (500g) unsweetened vanilla soy yogurt
- ·1 banana, sliced
- ·½ cup (60g) raspberries or blueberries
- ·¼ cup (30g) chopped pistachios
- ·¼ cup (30g) roasted unsalted sunflower seeds
- ·2 tbsp (30ml) honey
- ·1 tbsp (10g) hemp hearts for garnish
- ·1 tbsp (10g) cacao nibs for garnish

Directions

1.Divide the yogurt between two bowls. Evenly divide the banana, berries, pistachios, and sunflower seeds between the bowls.

2.Drizzle each bowl with 1 tablespoon of honey and top them with hemp hearts and cacao nibs. Serve.

 NUTRITIONAL VALUE

Kcal	Carbs	Protein	Total Fat	Sat. Fat	Cholesterol
394	55g	12g	18g	2g	0mg

CHOCOLATE BANANA CARAMEL PUDDING

SERVINGS

2

PREPARATION TIME

15 Mins

COOKING TIME

0 Mins

Ingredients

- ·1 ripe banana, cut into 1-inch (2,5cm) chunks
- ·1/8 cup (20g) cocoa powder
- ·1/8 cup (30g) of low-fat soy milk
- ·1 tbsp (12g) vanilla protein powder
- ·1 tbsp (15ml) caramel sauce
- ·1/8 tsp (0,5ml) vanilla extract
- ·Pinch of salt
- ·1 tbsp (10g) mini semisweet chocolate chips

Directions

1.In your blender or food processor, combine the bananas, cocoa powder, soy milk, protein powder, caramel sauce, vanilla, and salt, and blend or process until smooth.

2.Pour into 2 small cups, top each with the chocolate chips, and then serve.

 NUTRITIONAL VALUE

Kcal	Carbs	Protein	Total Fat	Sat. Fat	Cholesterol
164	25g	8g	4g	2g	1mg

30-DAY MEAL PLAN

DAY	BREAKFAST	LUNCH	DINNER	SNACKS/ DESSERTS
1	Tofu Scramble with Tomato and Spinach	Tofu with Chimichurri Sauce	Maple-Balsamic Pork Chops	Roasted Lentil Snack Mix
2	Tempeh Caprese Breakfast Sandwiches	Hawaiian Chicken Stir-Fry	Tofu and Root Vegetable Curry	Pumpkin Pie Fruit Leathers
3	Orange Apricot Muesli	Green Rice Salad with Tomatoes	Beef Burrito Skillet	Baked Tortilla Chips
4	Cinnamon Oat Bran Banana Pancakes	Brown Rice and Sweet Potato Pilaf	Baked Chicken Thighs with Leafy Greens	Chocolate Banana Caramel Pudding
5	Green Tea and Raspberry Smoothies	Beef and Broccoli Stir-Fry	Minestrone Florentine Soup	Garlicky Kale Chips
6	Nutty Rice Waffles	Lentil Pilaf	Roasted Haddock with Broccoli	Loaded Soy Yogurt Bowls
7	Asparagus Kale Frittata	Chili-Sautéed Tofu with Almonds	Curried Cauliflower-Lentil Soup	Sweet Potato Fries
8	Scrambled Egg Tacos	Chicken Thigh Cacciatore	Sirloin Steak with Root Vegetables	Maple-Walnut Pots de Crème
9	Berry, Kale, and Chia Smoothies	Mixed Berry Chicken Salad	Cod Scampi	Sesame-Garlic Edamame
10	Curried Farro Hot Cereal	Vietnamese Fish and Noodle Bowl	Curried Chickpea Stew	Peanut Butter and Chia Pudding
11	Amaranth and Date Porridge	Southwestern Millet-Stuffed Tomatoes	Haddock Tacos with Spicy Slaw	Mixed Vegetable Chips
12	Cranberry Orange Mixed Grain Granola	Fruited Quinoa Salad	Grilled Coffee-Rubbed Sirloin Steak	Tofu Mocha Mousse
13	Blueberry Almond Breakfast Bowl	Shrimp and Pineapple Lettuce Wraps	Chicken Alphabet Soup	Asparagus Fries
14	Pumpkin Oatmeal Smoothies	Cauliflower with Orzo and Black Beans	Dark Beer Beef Chili	Snowy Meringues with Berries

15	Honey Rice Pudding	Grilled Scallops with Gremolata	Baba Ghanoush Stew	Almond Cheesecake–Stuffed Apples
16	Tofu Scramble with Tomato and Spinach	Turkey and Mango Lettuce Wraps	Vegan Ratatouille	Peach Melba Frozen Yogurt Parfaits
17	Tempeh Caprese Breakfast Sandwiches	Butternut Squash, Bulgur, and Tempeh Burritos	Easy Pork Burgers	Mango Blood Orange Sorbet
18	Orange Apricot Muesli	Warm Soba and Tofu Salad	Salmon with Farro Pilaf	Roasted Lentil Snack Mix
19	Cinnamon Oat Bran Banana Pancakes	Steamed cod Rolls with Greens	Hearty Vegetable Stew	Pumpkin Pie Fruit Leathers
20	Green Tea and Raspberry Smoothies	Vegetable Lo Mein	Pork Cutlets with Fennel and Kale	Baked Tortilla Chips
21	Nutty rice Waffles	Lemon Garlic Mackerel	Mustard-Roasted Almond Chicken Tenders	Chocolate Banana Caramel Pudding
22	Asparagus Kale Frittata	Grilled Turkey and Veggie Kabobs	Vegetable and Barley Soup	Garlicky Kale Chips
23	Scrambled Egg Tacos	Spicy Pinto Bean rice Bowl	Lemon Tarragon Turkey Medallions	Loaded Soy Yogurt Bowls
24	Berry, Kale, and Chia Smoothies	Chicken with Mushroom Sauce	Chili-Sautéed Tofu with Almonds	Sweet Potato Fries
25	Curried Farro Hot Cereal	Balsamic Rosemary Chicken	Tuscan Fish Stew	Maple-Walnut Pots de Crème
26	Amaranth and Date Porridge	Roasted Tofu with Tomatoes and Peaches	Lemon Basil Pork Medallions	Sesame-Garlic Edamame
27	Cranberry Orange Mixed Grain Granola	Sesame-Crusted Tuna Steaks	Fall Vegetables Chicken Soup	Peanut Butter and Chia Pudding
28	Blueberry Almond Breakfast Bowl	Lemony Bulgur, Lentil, and Cucumber Salad	Sausage White Bean Stew	Mixed Vegetable Chips
29	Pumpkin Oatmeal Smoothies	Thai Soba Noodles with Spring Veggies	Honeyed Pork Tenderloin with Butternut Squash	Tofu Mocha Mousse
30	Honey Rice Pudding	Seitan Stir-Fry with Broccoli and Peas	Lentil Bolognese	Asparagus Fries

COOKING CONVERSION CHART

Volume Equivalents (Liquid)

US STANDARD	US STANDARD (OUNCES)	METRIC (APPROXIMATE)
2 tablespoons	1 fl. oz.	30 mL
¼ cup	2 fl. oz.	60 mL
½ cup	4 fl. oz.	120 mL
1 cup	8 fl. oz.	240 mL
1½ cups	12 fl. oz.	355 mL
2 cups or 1 pint	16 fl. oz.	475 mL
4 cups or 1 quart	32 fl. oz.	1 L
1 gallon	128 fl. oz.	4 L

Volume Equivalents (Dry)

US STANDARD	METRIC (APPROXIMATE)
⅛ teaspoon	0.5 mL
¼ teaspoon	1 mL
½ teaspoon	2 mL
¾ teaspoon	4 mL
1 teaspoon	5 mL
1 tablespoon	15 mL
¼ cup	59 mL
⅓ cup	79 mL
½ cup	118 mL
⅔ cup	156 mL
¾ cup	177 mL
1 cup	235 mL
2 cups or 1 pint	475 mL
3 cups	700 mL
4 cups or 1 quart	1 L
½ gallon	2 L
1 gallon	4 L

Oven Temperatures

FAHRENHEIT (F)	CELSIUS (C) (APPROXIMATE)
250	120
300	150
325	165
350	180
375	190
400	200
425	220
450	230

Weight Equivalents

US STANDARD	METRIC (APPROXIMATE)
½ ounce	15 g
1 ounce	30 g
2 ounces	60 g
4 ounces	115 g
8 ounces	225 g
12 ounces	340 g
16 ounces or 1 pound	455 g

CONCLUSION

Although some may feel restricted following a low-cholesterol diet, it doesn't mean eating healthy has to be tasteless. A wide variety of recipes and meal options are available to explore, where your meals will not only be flavorsome but heart-healthy. The key is to stay creative. Finding the right blend of ingredients that you enjoy can be a fun and rewarding experience.

The recipes in this cookbook have proven that they can be a delicious and varied way to accommodate individual taste preferences. This cookbook highlights the many different options available for those on a low-cholesterol diet. Recipes range from savory dinners to sweet indulgences that are sure to please and emphasize the importance of including heart-healthy ingredients. With this book as your guide, you can begin incorporating healthy and delicious meals into your new lifestyle.

It's worth noting that low-cholesterol diets require commitment, but it can be much easier with the right guidance. This cookbook is intended to help those who want to make a change by providing dietary advice and meal ideas that can be assembled in combination with original recipes or used as the basis for generating individual ideas. The recipes allow you to experiment with flavors and find new ingredients that could become your favorites. Eating healthy can bring many benefits, and these healthy recipes will help you get the most out of any low-cholesterol diet.

INDEX

Printed in Great Britain
by Amazon